SECURE FROM CRIME

How To Be Your Own Bodyguard

by

Craig Fox Huber
and
Don Paul

Path Finder Publications, 1296 E. Gibson Rd, E-301, Woodland, CA 95776
Dealer Phone Orders: 1-800-292-2702

ABOUT THE AUTHORS: Craig Fox Huber is a former marine, a weapons specialist, and a feature writer for various outdoor magazines. He spends mucht of his working time as one of the top bodyguards in the world. Don Paul, a law school graduate, is a former Green Beret and police officer. He's the author of several outdoor survival books.

Gratitude: To the manufacturers of home and personal defense devices. These people produce prodcuts and devices which preserve your life and freedom. For each one you buy, you lessen your chances of becoming a victim.

A.M.D.G.
Prayer: Before we publish, we bow our heads. *Lord, we want to rededicate our hearts to you as this book comes alive. Our lives are yours, our works are yours, and we acknowledge your Holy Scripture as standing forever. We believe our world is filled with crime because we've departed from your principles. We worship you, Father, and give you all the glory. Amen.*

Library of Congress Catalog Card Number: 92-81773

Publisher's Cataloging in Publication

Huber, Craig F., 1943- & Paul, Don, 1937-
    Secure from crime: How to be your own bodyguard / by Craig Fox Huber and Don Paul
    p. cm.
    Includes index
    ISBN 0-938263-16-1
    1. Crime Prevention. 2. Self Defense. 3. Self Defense for women. I. Paul, Don, 1937- II. Title
    HV7431.H83 1993   362.88
                           QBI92-20120

INTRODUCING...

QUICK READER BOOKS by PATH FINDER

<u>New-method, how-to books.</u>

To take a productive place in society, a writer has to focus on one goal. In this book, our goal is: **To protect your life.** That's what a bodyguard does for a client. Your bodyguard isn't just any bodyguard, either. He earns about a thousand a day guarding some of the richest royalty in the world, not only in the U.S., but during their travels all over the globe. Huber is high-ticket because he's best. That's why we asked him to write for us.

At Path Finder, we have a different publishing philosophy. We take our best shot at going <u>beyond any other knowledge in a given field.</u> We explain, in simple, easy-to-understand detail, the new methods we've discovered. To do that, we use independent editors and electronic manuscript scrubbers to make sure <u>we're crystal clear, easy and quick to read.</u> We care about saving your time. That's what we did in this book. Though the information is life-saving and critical, the text is written and specially formatted for speed reading. Maybe it's choppy, but <u>we're sure you'll get it---fast.</u> Our electronic scrubbers report:

At the sub-vocalization reading rate of less than 600 wpm, you should complete this whole book in 1 hour, 29 minutes, not including box additions, which we provide for concentration relief. After scrubbing, we achieved reading-ease parity with Hemingway's short stories. We average under 1.4 syllables per word. Our average sentence: Under 15 words. We cut graphic description paragraphs by more than half with our illustrations.

Path Finder began over 10 years ago. We first invented a way to keep you from getting lost in the woods without using a map; it was called, <u>Never Get lost. The Green Beret's Compass Course,</u>   Over 25,000 copies are in print. After that, we added to our book list and widened our distribution. We published:

<u>Everybody's Outdoor Survival Guide</u>
<u>Great Livin' in Grubby Times</u> best selling survival book.
<u>Everybody's Knife Bible</u> over 30,000 copies!
<u>24 + Ways to Use Your Hammock in the Field.</u>
<u>How to Write a Book in 53 Days.</u> We teach our audience how to write as fast and efficiently as this book can be read.

i

We develop and write about new ideas and outdoor methods. We're the innovative people who wrote about outdoor know-how and discovered:

√A two-ounce, 30¢ wilderness bed for sleeping above ground.

√The modification for your hunting knife sheath which enables you to see the floor of a jungle or woods at night.

√A new shooting system that gives you super bullet placement, day or night.

√A new cold-weather survival method to keep you alive.

√A guide to water purification for any survivalist.

√How to use animals to double your survive-ability.

√Wind reading for super long distance shooting.

√Green Beret team concepts applied to survival groups so you can enjoy the ultimate life-style outdoors.

All our books have gone into multiple editions. Most major outdoor magazines have reviewed our books and our systems have been adopted by many outdoor organizations.

We publish only in paperback. <u>Once you own any of our books, you can order a new, updated copy for half price, no questions asked.</u>

In this book, one large chapter is **for women only.** To make this book's price fair, we include a discount coupon on other titles.

(See the order coupons in the back of this book.)

This is **the book you can't live without.** Huber and Paul believe you could die without this information.   Huber is a highly experienced bodyguard and Paul is a former Green Beret. Both give away trade secrets. We may not have a war against crime in this country, but for sure, criminals are waging a war against us. Surviving a criminal attack takes two critical skills. You need to be your own bodyguard------always alert to danger and capable of handling it. Also, you need to develop a tactical outlook to live safely in today's crime-infested, concrete jungles.

One more thing---

We wrote this because: More than any constitutional right a criminal has, you have a right to live your life in peace---free of danger. <u>We're sure that many of our readers will save both property and lives as a result of owning this book.</u> If you escape being a victim because of what you learned here, please let us know.

How to stay. . .
SECURE FROM CRIME
How To Be Your Own Bodyguard

Table of Contents

b

Stay . . .

SECURE FROM CRIME

How To Be Your Own Bodyguard

by
Craig Fox Huber
and
Don Paul

INTRODUCTION

Have you noticed? People who plan for emergencies rarely need to deal with them. The fellow with two spare tires, an extra fan belt, and a small tool box drives all the way across the country without a problem. Meanwhile, the guy without a spare tire has a flat, his fan belt breaks, and his engine overheats. He doesn't have a quarter for a phone call. This isn't the first time, either. He has never learned:

"Fail to prepare, and you prepare to fail."

"Be prepared." For what? Violent crime; that's what. Our world just isn't a safe place anymore. Therefore, **to survive in this society, you either have to hire a full time bodyguard, or learn to be your own.**

It used to be that courts were more concerned with the rights of citizens than civil rights of criminals. Lawbreakers paid severe penalties. House burglars knew that if someone was home, they would likely have to deal with Mr. Colt. Murderers who were caught and convicted were executed. Unfortunately, those days are gone. G. Gordon Liddy states the case well in an article for *Forbes Magazine* titled, "Security."

"There are essentially two kinds of people in this world, and they can be distinguished easily by their reaction to life-threatening situations such as the invasion of one's home. All resort to prayer. But it is by the text of their prayers ye shall know them. For some it's a version of `God, please don't let them find me,' then when found, `God, please don't let them hurt me.' Sometimes the plea is for a miracle: `God, please let the police get here in time!' Such persons have elected to be life's victims and, indeed, only God can help them.

There are others, however, who've chosen not to be victims, and to whom it has occurred that God may, from time to time, be busy on another line and it might be prudent to do the necessary thing to protect themselves. Their prayer, left on the divine answering machine, is for the intruder: `May God have mercy on your soul.' This article is for them."

You'll begin to understand crime and its effect in our society when you look at it as a disease. **Consider criminals as germs and viruses.** Our courts and penal system limit the cure, so the disease spreads and flourishes. If doctors worked under the same restraints as police do today, they couldn't practice medicine; germs and viruses would have rights! No health official could kill mosquitoes until *after* they had bitten and infected you. You couldn't take penicillin until *after* an infection had done irreparable damage. Even with infections roaring in your body, only limited amounts of cure could be applied.

Today, the criminal germs have the upper hand. The police can do little until *after* a crime has been committed. Even if a criminal *is* caught and sent to prison (for curing), our system pampers him. What **is** jail, anyway? It's a place where germs meet, get shelter, a bed, and three meals a day, all at your expense. Jail is a punishment only if you don't have anything in common with the people who are already there.

Do you really have to prepare now? On September 3rd, 1992, during *Larry King Live*, L.A. police officer Ted Briseno (one of those accused of excessive force against Rodney King) told the nation, "We knew there would be a riot in Los Angeles after the trial whether there was a conviction or acquittal." Were citizens protected? As the riots began, the police retreated. The National Guard showed up---without ammunition. Mayor Bradley and Jesse Jackson spoke out apologetically with exculpatory statements about the poor rioters. Even more incredible, good citizens couldn't purchase guns or ammunition!

Even in the absence of a riot, crime is on the upswing everywhere. You'd better develop a personal defense plan for yourself and your home immediately. Take some simple and basic precautions; otherwise, plan on becoming a victim. Get ready now; later, when some germ attacks or invades, will be too late. If you want to *win during* the inevitable battle, you'll have to prepare *now*.

To develop a correct mind set about crime and how it relates to you, try to understand this horrible news. **You're at war!** Seldom in history have neighboring subcultures with different value systems and ideals co-existed in peace. Early Americans shared a common set of values; today's Americans don't. Various colors and subcultures steal from and brutalize everyone---then rationalize it with bitterness and hatred. Drugs eradicate any remaining shred of fear or dread of consequence in a criminal virus who wants to attack you. Values in some Americans come from a welfare mentality developed over generations. "What's yours is mine (my entitlement) because I'm poor."

> **PROPOSED NEW LAW:** If you're convicted of a felony, you get no government welfare, housing allowance, or food stamps. We agree to let you stay in prison until you can learn a trade and prove you can support yourself when you get out.

So---somebody out there wants to attack you or your family. Your property, your body, or your life mean nothing to these people. The criminal surrounds himself with a subculture in which rebellion against the law makes him a hero. Fueled by a deep-seated resentment and bitterness, the compulsion to have overwhelms.

They already hate you. Understand this: It isn't a personal problem they have with you; it only appears that way. They hate, period. Witness the violent deaths in the news. Hundreds of others who might not make the news because they don't die are beaten, robbed, raped, or victimized. For how much? Oftentimes, for a few bucks. Like a car burglar who causes hundreds of dollars in vehicle damage to rip off a CB radio worth $25 in most pawn shops, the amount they steal isn't important. But the act of stealing inflates their self image, so they keep on finding new victims. Those victims never had a chance to decide whether they wanted to be at war. Neither do you. Any time another country or gang attacks you, you're in a war whether you like it or not.

In order to survive this war, take advice from those with military experience. Craig Huber was a Marine and is now one of the top personal security consultants in the world. Don Paul was a Green Beret and has written two successful books on survival. He worked for years as a police officer in San Diego. Both want you to know:

<u>The best way to fight a war is to learn about your enemy,</u>
<u>and make your battle plans accordingly.</u>

Who's your enemy? Scripture teaches us how to know a man or woman. It says, "By their fruits shall you know them." What are gangs producing? Why does crime exist? Where does all the violence come from? Simply this: Lack of self image. It's the same in all mankind. It's the compulsion to raise ourselves up above others. Self image demands that A. we make something of ourselves, B. that we acquire things so *it looks like* we made something out of ourselves, or C. that we win in sports, at work, or in other achievements so *we can say* we made something out of ourselves. Different subcultures put different values on achievement. To a yuppie, it's how much money he earns. To a criminal virus, it's like a bullfight. You see how big a yuppie you can blow away or how big the score is on the goods you steal. Expressed by a gang member in October 1992 on the Jerry Springer television talk show, "You got to earn your respect." Many gang members believe the greatest honor they can earn is to die for their colors.

AUTO INSURANCE FOR DRIVERS THEREFORE, VICTIM INSURANCE FOR CRIMINALS

In almost every state in the union, auto insurance is mandatory. Lawmakers have devised several methods of enforcement. Uninsured drivers pay severe penalties.

Statistics show that convicted criminals are likely to commit new crimes, yet they need carry <u>no victim insurance.</u>

If a driver can't drive without insurance because of the <u>possibility of accident</u>, then no convict should go free without insurance because of the <u>high probability of his committing a new crime.</u>

Can you coexist peacefully in a society in which most of the criminal element is unpunishable and goes unchecked? In James, Chapter 4:1, the Bible says, "What causes fights and quarrels among you? Don't they come from your desires that battle within you?" God knows: The war exists because we want one pleasure and some criminal germ wants the same thing. Edward James Olmos, star of

4

Miami Vice and the feature film, *American Me*, said, "The newest craze isn't gangs; it's random violence . . ." The random violence is coming from a mal-adjusted psychopath who thinks of himself as a nobody and is looking for an upper-type thrill. Thus the killing. If you ask, you'll learn: Hardened criminals think it's a real rush to break into a house, steal a car, grab a purse and run, or kill somebody. Succeed, and their peers consider them a hero. Fail, and they get acceptance and appreciation for trying to buck the system.

This is the new street ethic: "Whatever you're not strong enough to keep belongs to me." Is there an effective deterrent for a criminal? Yes---fear of pain, injury, or perhaps death. These are deterrents you'll have to supply when you're faced with a crime; to a criminal germ or virus, our criminal justice system is a joke.

Given attitudes engendered by hatred, fueled by government give-aways and the low self image welfare gives the taker, how does most crime take place? Against <u>targets of opportunity</u>. You, or your property becomes somebody's prey because attacking or stealing is convenient. The germs and attackers were already committed to the act long before they picked on you to be a victim. Seldom do they see themselves as bad for taking your property. Long years of government giving has taught them that taking from you is merely another way of acquiring an entitlement.

MARTIAL TO CIVIL LAW SLIDE ON RIGHTS

Who should get more rights—-criminals or the citizens they oppress? Is our civil, as opposed to martial, law system working to provide us with a safe environment in which to pursue our inalienable rights? If not, why not martial law? Too stringent?

Then how about a law system in between the extremes of martial and civil? If the function of a law system is to provide a safe atmosphere for society, why not control civil rights on a scale? Let's modify civil law to become increasingly martial as crime increases in any given area. Civil rights for the accused must decrease in a high-crime area. Otherwise, society cannot remain balanced, and criminal anarchy will eventually rule.

Where do we face threats? Everywhere! We're at risk in our homes, in the family car, on vacation, at work and school, and anytime we are exposed to the public. Anytime we fly on a commercial airline or

5

travel on public transportation, we're at risk. Whenever we drive in any major U.S. city we're in danger of being caught in a violent situation.

Now that you understand what you're faced with, perhaps you can apply the great bodyguard maxim. Guard your own body and possessions the same way a bodyguard would guard a rich client:
"Don't get out of trouble. Keep out of trouble."

This book shows you how to do that. We'll reduce your chances of being attacked or robbed. The tricks and tips in this book teach you to do what most good soldiers do—minimize your risk and carry on with your life's mission.

Even with making your chances minimal, you still may find yourself in a battle. Because it might happen, we'll show you how to **defeat the enemy**---decisively!

Alfredo found God and now works as a manager of a retail store in Chula Vista, California. He said, "I blew six guys away when I was a drug dealer. But I can only remember three of them because I was too high." Though he works in the U.S, he lives in Tijuana. Why? It's safer. Most of the bad guys moved north across the border where criminal justice is not as harsh.

GENERAL DEFENSE PLAN AGAINST CRIME
In the movie, *The Untouchables,* Sean Connery (1930's Irish street cop) twice asks Kevin Costner (as Elliot Ness, FBI agent against prohibition), **"What are you prepared to do?"** The first time was during a conversation on the street. The second time, Connery was on the floor of his home in a pool of blood, and it was his last question. We're asking you the same question now. The toughest difficulty you'll have to overcome is with your own mind-set. This is something you can do, and must do. We lay it out for you. You'll find it immensely easier to develop an anti-victim mentality when you understand how the enemy thinks and how his sick mind developed a total disregard for your rights.

The principles in this book will teach you to plan your defense, develop an attitude against being a victim, and therefore live in much improved safety and peace.

6

Chapter 1

PERSONAL DEFENSE MEASURES

Study the job of bodyguarding and you'll learn: Clients who've expired don't write checks. If you want to get paid, you have to keep your client breathing. What's the best way to succeed at your job? Anticipate and plan, or *planticipate*. Look for trouble, then avoid it. Anytime you have to pull your weapon, smack an intruder or drive like a New York cabbie to get away, you probably screwed up.

Today, many areas of the United States are much like Vietnam during the war. We own it during the day, but the night belongs to criminals. Many neighborhoods are no longer safe. You would be amazed at the number of attacks on "ordinary, honest citizens" that occur in places you'd think a sensible person would avoid. I'm sure those victims who survived wish they had done things differently.

You can learn from their mistakes. For example, instead of visiting a convenience store after 11:00 PM, do without a gallon of milk or a candy bar. The incidents of rape and assault near convenience stores, especially those within easy walking distance of coed college dorms, is extremely high. If you need something after hours, try to find a store frequented by the local police on their coffee breaks. Feel free to introduce yourself. If they know you and consider you a "friend," they are more likely to respond to your call for help. Also, in a violent confrontation on your property, probably at night, they're less likely to confuse you with a perp (short for perpetrator, one who commits a crime).

7

The 24 hour Auto-Tellers are just too dangerous to use after dark. It's just too easy for a perp with a gun to persuade you to rob your bank on his behalf. We think you should avoid these. If you must---a hand-held spotlight or a five-cell flashlight is better because a hiding perp thinks you're a cop. Remember, there's safety in numbers. Wait in your car alone until a line of people are there. Lock your car! Carry a weapon! Some perps will ambush you as you return. They either hide in your car or wait for you in nearby shadows.

Other areas are dangerous, too. Be particularly cautious in all parking lots, community parks, construction sites, amusement parks, carnivals, poorly lit streets, pawn shop and X-rated movie areas, red light districts, hangouts for drug peddlers and users, areas with a vagrant populace (like beach parking lots), and areas with a high concentration of derelict buildings. Any one of these places could well be the last place you visit.

FELONS, NO MORE ACCESS TO PUBLIC LANDS
If a judge can issue a restraining order to avoid a potential problem, why not restrict felons from certain public lands as well as private property owned by others? The idea is to give citizens freedom to take a walk in a public park without fear and to make trespass a crime. How to enforce? ID checks by patrol with NCIC computer reports over the radio.

Hospitals are now hazardous to your health in one specific area—-parking lots. After dark, weirdoes just love the target-rich environment offered by shift-changing nurses. The thugs 'n drugs crowd like to pick on doctors and their vehicles. Visit hospitals during the early afternoon hours whenever possible.

WATCH OUT IN ELEVATORS
Your health and safety both will appreciate you using the stairs. Older public elevators are dangerous. If you step into one from the lobby and select an upper floor, it may still go down to answer the call of the thief or pervert lurking in the basement or underground parking. When you're alone, they get you. Solution: Step in by yourself from the lobby. Push, B, L, and 5 (Basement Lobby, and any upper floor), then step back out into the lobby. On the elevator location indicator on top of the main doors, watch it go down to the basement and come back up. When it stops at the lobby empty the second time, climb aboard to go up. If your elevator stops before you get where you're going and a suspicious thug gets in, step off. Stand near the operating panel in case

you need help. As soon as the perp leaves after a purse snatch, hit the alarm button. It makes him run so witnesses know whom to identify.

<u>WOMEN ALONE</u>
Purse snatching isn't particularly profitable, but it's popular because it's easy and simple. You don't need a brain to grab a purse and run. Think about the psychological state of the perpetrator. Many street robbers are just coming down off their latest drug binge. To say the least, it makes them moody. They don't have time to figure out a complicated crime. They need—-<u>now</u>, and women's purses are everywhere, so they grab and go.

Subway perps often stand near their victim and grab the purse just before the doors close. The perp walks free as the robbed victim moves down the track behind closed doors. Recently, two perps in Los Angeles drove along close to the sidewalk and grabbed a purse belonging to a 94-year-old woman. They dragged her over a hundred feet to a horrible death before getting away. On the street, it happens all the time; that's why we teach you to walk against traffic. Some germ hero can't hang out a car window and grab from behind you.

Hide your purse! Don't carry your house keys and ID there, either. If they get your purse with ID and keys, they'll pick you clean at your home address without having to break in. You put your life at risk when you dangle bait (your purse) in front of a drug addict. Attach a long carrying strap to your purse and carry it over your shoulder, under your coat. If you're carrying something valuable, and it looks as if you're being stalked, you can ditch your purse in any mail box and get it back from the post office later. Also, forget carrying an expensive bag. Buy a nylon belt purse (also called a fanny pack) and buckle it around your waist. If you don't feel comfortable without a purse, spread most of your money and credit cards around. Inside shirt and coat pockets make good stash places. So do the tops of socks.

Statistics show, you're especially vulnerable just as you step onto the street or parking lot. Don't get out of your car without scanning your mirrors and taking a good look around. Husbands, be your wife's LIFO, (Last In, First Out). She gets into the car first to drive while you scan the perimeter. When you arrive, check first for potential dangers before you get out of the car to secure her safe exit.

Women, especially alone, are a <u>prime target</u> for robbery and assault. They're perceived to be weaker, and supposed to be easier to scare. Besides, the perp worries less about getting hurt. Also, many perps turn to crime because they had dysfunctional relationships with the only parent around---the mother. Psychologists tell us of one prevalent reason: Aggression transfer. The 30 something husband leaves the nest for a 20 year-old lollipop. The 10 year old boy he leaves with mom looks and talks just like his father---at whom mom is really miffed. So the boy catches all the flak the mother really wants to heap on the father. When the boy grows up, any woman is a potential scapegoat. The added vengeful power trip of rape is an added lure.

Thus, no matter where you are, you'll have to become more security conscious. Lock your doors everywhere. Don't make unnecessary trips anywhere. Don't go into major cities without a companion. Stay behind privacy curtains at home, and tinted windows in your car. Finally, watch your telephone security. Give out no information; talk to no strangers; list no phone numbers; and, don't allow strangers into your space.

If your car breaks down, **do not** accept help from strangers. The slightest social contact with some men who stop to help a lady can be trouble. Once your car is fixed, they think you owe them.

<u>ARMED MUGGING---THE MORE PERSONAL TOUCH</u>
Reconsider the psychological state of the mugger. He's just dropping down off a drug high. You think you had a bad day? This is the worst. So, he pulls a knife or pistol, aims it at you and says, "Give me your wallet!"

Don't respond aggressively. That makes perps horribly mad. The idea is not to die. Instead, buy life by cooperating as best you can. Be gracious and say something like: "No problem, take it all."

Don't even think about argument. Insure your life with whatever you can give him. Make sure you have something to give—at least a $10, better a $20. Don't carry credit cards with your money. If your credit card is in your wallet, you may get shot. Fences pay higher prices for cards which can't be canceled right away, and dead people can't cancel credit cards.

Credit card companies could alleviate the problem by putting up a special reward for any perp who steals a card and murders the victim. Few perps have any loyal friends. Also, ask your credit card company for a personal code number or a phony name (like a CB handle) only you can use when charging. When you're real name is Donna Marie but the computer knows you as Ima Shoptil Idrop, nobody but you can use the card. With such a system in operation, we can can save hundreds of lives. One other system now in operation is the photo credit card. You send in a photograph of yourself and the credit card comes back with your picture on it. Nobody else can use it.

IF YOU'RE TAKEN HOSTAGE

Comply with the criminal's demands until your first opportunity to escape or attack. Just do what they tell you until you get your chance. More victims wind up getting hurt when they don't resist.

Suppose your captor uses you as a shield while shooting at anyone else. Grab his gun hand with both of yours. If you get his pistol in both your hands, collapse his wrist inward so his weapon points back at him. If you continue to twist inward, he'll have to let go.

RECOGNIZING TROUBLE ON THE HORIZON

"Not long ago I spent an afternoon with a good friend. He's an experienced observer and hunter who seldom lacks sensitivity to his surroundings. One day, he and his wife invited me to dinner at a great new Chinese restaurant. We drove in his $65,000 gray Mercedes.

In an area of closed businesses and run-down housing units, a motley looking crew of apparent miscreants looked us over from their corner at a traffic light. After a short discussion, four of the group started in our direction. I hit the door locks. 'Possible trouble on the right,' I said to my host. He gave no reaction—-not even a glance.

While drawing my licensed handgun from my hip pocket, I noticed the light was still red. No help there. The approaching foursome split up. One pair came towards the right front door while the other pair moved around to the rear of the car. All four had hands thrust into coat pockets.

'We really ought to be moving along,' I warned.

'No hurry; our reservation isn't until 8:30.'

The group still on the corner was busy looking in all directions. Another pair stepped off the curb against the 'DON'T WALK' sign. They paused in the roadway where they could prevent us from making a right turn on the red.

Checking both directions and seeing no oncoming traffic I reached over, locked my hand on the steering wheel and stepped down on my friend's accelerator foot. Amidst the gang's obscenities, we shot across the intersection. When I eased up about halfway down the next block, my friend was flabbergasted."

Even though a genius, the driver failed to do what most police departments now recommend: <u>Turn your perception knobs up</u>. With his wife along, in a sleazy section of a major, East Coast city, in a car that screams '**I have money**,' he didn't even carry a weapon. Even for great food, a bad neighborhood is scarcely worth the risk.

Here's the point. Most educated people wouldn't think of walking in a South American jungle at night. But, as anyone with jungle experience will tell you, <u>those jungles are much safer than our city streets.</u> If you want to be secure from crime, you have to assess the dangers out there realistically. We can't stress this enough: **The best defense against violence is to avoid places where violence is most likely to occur.**

<u>COURTS MUST TAKE JUDICIAL NOTICE OF SIXTH SENSE</u>

Citizens are not allowed to use more force than that which they <u>perceive</u> as being used on them. Key word here is <u>"perceive."</u> If the criminal had previous a conviction or a previous arrest, then the citizen's assessment of danger was correct, and the danger perceived was real. Therefore, no crime in shooting a perpetrator.

Also, take advantage of the fact that you may have a friend with you. Whether you're walking on the street or driving in any kind of vehicle, warn each other of potentially dangerous situations. If you suspect anybody, <u>watch his hands</u>. Tell your companion about your suspicions. Identify the location of the trouble so both of you know what you're talking about. As you travel, you move towards 12:00 o'clock, with three on your right and nine on your left. So---suppose you're being followed by a shady looking character off to your right. You say, "There's a creep following us at five o'clock 15 yards out."

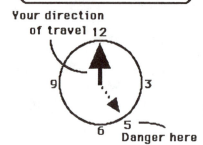

CLOCK CIRCLE TO IDENTIFY DANGER

Your direction of travel 12

9   3

6   5
Danger here

WHAT CAN YOU DO ABOUT THE DANGER OUT THERE?

Probably, the **DefCon** system may work best. Short for **Defense Condition**, it takes into account the seriousness of the danger, the probability of a crime occurring, (consider the neighborhood and your surroundings), the proximity of the suspected perpetrator, and the suspect's movement and appearance. If the guy looks weird or out of place, assume he is trouble. Many macho people show off their tatoos and grow gross looking facial hair; their appearance is a display of rebellion. You need to decide if they are dangerous. You really do have a sixth sense. If the situation feels bad, it probably is.

You have tasks to do as soon as you sense danger—-you prepare in stages. Maybe you sense danger when you can't really see or hear anything. That's your first notice, your warning order. Size things up. How many of the enemy? Are they focused on you? Are they within 10 yards?

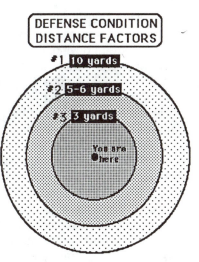

If the answer to any of the above questions indicates trouble, you go to **DefCon 1**. That means you get control of your weapon and get it ready, address the problem by giving it your full and obvious attention, and look for a way out. If your weapon is a handgun, then your hand is on it. Watch these people. Also check behind you for a silent partner. Choose an escape route, or at least a place that gives you a defensive advantage. Perhaps it's a crowded store you can duck into, or some men in uniform you can ask for help.

DefCon 2 occurs after you have made tactical moves to avoid the problem, and the problem persists. It's now 5-6 yards away and closing in on you. You're closer to an escape route. Maybe you've moved towards help. You've double-surveyed your area 360° to check for additional trouble. Your plan of defense is clear, and you're getting ready. Your weapon is now ready. If it's a handgun, it may still be hidden, but the safety is off and you're prepared to fire.

At 3 yards, with things getting progressively worse, you'll have to make an offensive move. Take a stand. Get control of the situation. You can say, "Stop right there! You people are scaring me. If you want to avoid severe pain, turn around and leave right now!" This is **DefCon 3**, and the next step is shoot. Once you've issued a warning, you have a right to be afraid. Fear for your life is grounds to spray gas, attack with a non-shooting weapon, or let lead fly. When all your DefCon 3 options have been used, go to war. Win decisively. Don't wound or try to disable; shoot to kill. Make your first shot count. Your second shot, (in the air) should be your warning shot.

Most law enforcement agencies have an unwritten policy regarding the use of wounding (to disable) violent subjects. <u>Don't!</u> If an individual is armed and posing a threat to anyone, <u>shoot to kill</u>! Officers involved in fatal shootings are instructed to testify to the fact they were shooting to "incapacitate" or to "neutralize" a subject or threat. Death usually does that.

<u>STAYING AWARE</u>
Knowledge and awareness of your surroundings are critical ingredients of any self-defense plan. <u>Always pay attention to what is going on.</u> When driving, listen to the news. A police scanner in your car can warn you of trouble ahead. When at home listen for telltale sounds indicating trouble. A squeaky door, floorboards creaking, or the sound of broken glass should alert you.   In an enclosed space, learn a trick from karate instructors: Don't stare ahead at one point; soften your focus. Train yourself to see everything 180° in front of you.

Don't situate yourself so you look into the sun outdoors or into bright lights indoors. The idea is to observe; not to be seen. Don't turn up your television, stereo or car radio so loud that you can't hear what is going on. The idea is to hear; not to make a lot of noise. Headphones make you deaf to your surroundings and kill your ability to sense danger. You can let your guard down in one area of the country without a problem, but the same relaxation could get you quickly killed just a few miles down the road.

Besides being cautious, show restraint in dress. Don't display wealth or expensive jewelry.   Wear gloves over your rings until you're out of sight of the casual observer, the parking lot attendant, the cab driver, or the ticket taker at the opera. Many of those people sell information. They're part time, hired for one night only, and sometimes go after those kinds of jobs just for the extra bucks they can make from the information they pass along.

To stay less of a target, develop a lower profile. Don't buy season tickets to the opera or ball game in your name. Certainly, don't have tickets sent to your home address. The list of season ticket holders is frequently sold for six cents a name. The person who goes to the opera every Thursday is an easy mark for house burglars. Buy tickets in the name of the company for which you work and take delivery elsewhere than your home—-your business address or your mail box.

MAIL AND ADDRESS SECURITY
Your home address should appear on none of your personal identification. Get a privately owned mail box (Mail Boxes Etc.) or at least a post office box address and use that on your driver's license and vehicle registration. If it isn't that way now, fill out a form and change it. Thus, whoever steals your wallet doesn't get your home address. Use the same mailing address on your car keys. With name and true home address on your key ring, loss or theft makes it easy for thieves to invade your home. Likewise, use your mail box address on baggage labels at airports. Why? Baggage handlers have been known to sell information to house burglars---who would just love to know you'll be gone for a few weeks.

More and more, people shop by phone with a credit card across state lines as state sales taxes increase. (Some states collect no sales tax on out-of-state deliveries.) Never give your home address to any stranger, especially over the phone. Take delivery at your mail box address.

PHONE SECURITY
Every phone conversation you have with friends should include an, " I'm OK" code message. For example, "Buddy's doing fine," means: Everything's all right. Without that being said over the phone, it means, "I'm in trouble and I need help right away." Now you can warn someone without saying anything an assailant could construe as a tip-off.

Also, be careful over the cellular phone. Many scanners can be programmed to cellular channels so criminal eaves droppers can routinely listen in. Some sell information.

VARY YOUR ACTIVITY

Don't establish easily observed patterns of travel and activity. Interested high school drop out thieves keep notes on your arrival and departures. Don't drive the same route every day; take as many different routes as possible to work and school. Leave and return at different times. Computers and modems are creating new home employment opportunities. Any time you can work at home instead of the office, you decrease your exposure.

Discussing your wealth with strangers or casual acquaintances is very poor security. Referencing your Mercedes, your summer home, or 'Daddy's little ole factory' are all poor choices for casual conversation with any but your closest friends. While we're at it, don't reserve any parking space anywhere in your own name. Use a code name, the same way you should on your credit cards. For the management staff at Disneyland, for example, who just made millions of dollars, I recommend labelling the spaces with Mickey Mouse, Goofey etc, and rotating the names every so often. Otherwise, anybody with a pair of binoculars can find out the bosses' license numbers, trace the car to the house, or set up a kidnap while the car is in transit.

Engrave everything you own. Fences pay less for traceable property. Thieves have been known to leave engraved goods alone. Also, police catch thieves and recover thousands in stolen goods. If engraved, you get them back and the prosecution's case is stronger. If not, they go to a police auction and the perp frequently goes free.

Use the same sting technique on any employee who is supposed to shield you from unwanted visitors. Hire a detective to try a bribe. The detective agency operator goes into your office and says to your secretary, "Look, I don't have an appointment, but could I pay you $50 to let me see the boss?"

Trust nobody. Today, many police departments hire bad apples. With all the drug money around, temptation is tremendous. In Kailua, Oahu, Hawaii, the police department discovered several officers connected with burglars and stolen property. Some resigned, and the newspapers never published the names of others. In San Diego, an attorney who was president of the local Bar Association was indicted for receiving stolen property. He apparently was fencing for several thieves, many of whom were his clients.

16

Never give a parking lot attendant or auto service man your key complete ring. With the parking lot attendant, only the ignition key is necessary. It's far better to arrange to park the car yourself and keep your keys. House keys left in trust with your neighbor get no ID tag. An enterprising thief in your neighbor's home would pocket your key for future use, of course.

DAYTIME BURGLARY, OWNER DECOYED
In the "Gypsy Scenario," the thieves leave town before you even discover the theft. They might hit three or four homes in an area and then move on fifty or a hundred miles before discovery. It goes something like this: You're out in your front yard raking leaves. A friendly, presentable-looking individual, quite often an attractive young women, approaches and says, "Hi. I'm so-and-so and I'm doing a survey for the board of education. Is your wife home? I promise I'm not selling anything and I will take less than five minutes of her time."

If your wife is not home, or if she comes out of the house to speak to the young lady, a signal of some kind tells the young lady's accomplice to enter the house on the opposite side and spend five minutes gathering up valuables. When the young lady gets a signal that her accomplice has departed, she leaves.

When at home in your yard, keep all doors locked. Have a cordless phone in your yard with you. Head toward the house. If she leaves quickly or suspiciously, call 911 with a description. Give the vehicle make, (if any), the license number, and a description of your interviewer. Then wait for the cops to come and search the rest of your house for a hidden burglar. Warn them, "Watch it, I believe there's a burglar in this house and he may be armed. Would you search while I wait outside?"

Be careful about going into your house if things are not as you left them. An open front door into your house may draw you in to a burglary in progress, and 50% of these turn out to be violent. The same with a car. If the doors are open and you know you locked them, be careful. Call for help and don't touch anything.

There are three time frames to be considered in any defense plan. These are *before, during, and after.* The police are not responsible for providing any particular citizen a blanket of security "before" a crime is committed. Rarely can the police arrive "during" a crime.

17

What's the bottom line? They take reports—*after*. Sometimes, that doesn't work too well. In many areas, county sheriffs and city police don't cooperate. Even though you live in the city, police won't take a report on a theft you think occurred in the county. Sheriffs' crime reports often don't filter in to police information output. Political infighting and bitterness between elected officials puts you more at risk than ever. Witness L.A. We understand they plan to burn it again.

The *before* and *during* time frames of a crime are up to you. Almost always, the police handle the *after* when they write up the report. The steps you take *before* a crime happens may make the difference between your living unmolested in peace or becoming a victim. Use the time you have *before* to plan what will happen *during*. Once you formulate your plan and practice, your life should go along smoothly with little interference from the criminal germs and viruses around you.

One of the great things about America is the entrepreneurial spirit which produces so many solutions to so many problems. When we researched home security, we were amazed at how many firms make good products that fill a need---the need we have to be secure in our homes. Path Finder wishes to thank those home security products manufacturers who supported our research efforts and sold us great products to test and endorse.

Chapter 2

FORTIFYING YOUR CASTLE

Burglary! It's **big business**. In California alone, burglars stole 864 million dollars worth of property in 1991. When police announce they have just broken a burglary ring operating for the last five years, take note. Many small American businesses fold after operating for less than a year, so a five-year run is a success story. When you factor in the cost of police efforts to put burglars out of business, either the burglars are doing something right, or the criminal justice system isn't . .

The average home in America is a pushover for any amateur burglar. Approximately 50% of burglars enter through an unlocked door or window. Others come in via an open garage. Your house may be locked, but if the garage is open, the burglar enters, shuts the garage door, and uses the owner's tools to break in through a wall. From **Armor Garage Door Locks**, 800-845-7769, you can purchase remote controlled dead bolt locks for your garage door. But, **don't** remote these to the same frequency as your garage door opener.

You can make your house absolutely impregnable, when you make your house just a little harder to break into than your neighbors' houses, you've probably eliminated 90% of possible break-ins. Contrary to other kinds of crime, a lot of burglary occurs during school hours. Watch the rate climb when teachers go on strike.

WHO OWNS YOUR PROPERTY?

Ownership of anything is determined by who has dominion and control over the thing. You don't own property because it's registered in your name or because you pay the taxes on it. Anyone can take it from you if there is no restraining force and no fear of punishment. Maybe the real owner of your property is a neighborhood gang.

IF YOU MOVE TO A NEW AREA

One of the best ways to reduce risk at home is to be careful in your choice of neighborhoods. A cul de sac neighborhood with only one access street is far less appealing to criminals. A neighborhood with security fencing and a guarded entrance is helpful. The high risk for attack by professional house breakers is between 9:00 in the morning and 2:00 in the afternoon. That's one reason we like **Maxwell alarm** screens. They prohibit window entry. People are generally at work or at school during these hours and a delivery or service van elicits little suspicion from the neighbors. An area where some folks have retired and remained in place is a great deal better than one where all the adults are away all day. Retired folks grew up during a time when honesty and property rights were respected. They don't have a regular schedule to keep, love to walk around the neighborhood at odd times, and seem to notice most everything going on.

Moving into a new neighborhood with the NEIGHBORHOOD WATCH program is a step in the right direction as far as home defense planning is concerned. There, neighbors band together and keep track of strange cars and the even stranger people who drive them. They each keep a roster of neighbors' phone numbers so they can check on visitors or intruders. In pairs, they often walk through the neighborhood at night to check things out.

Other considerations would include: a neighborhood away from the main stream of urban traffic, but one that is not remote from police, fire department, ambulance and other emergency services. The house itself shouldn't be secluded. It should be easily seen from the street by passing police patrols and easily observed by your immediate neighbors.

FORTIFICATION

Just in the federal budget, defense should be an on-going item in your personal monthly budget. Spend so much per month for groceries, so much for defense, etc. It's the price of peace. Thus, your house

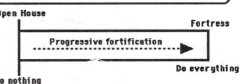

keeps getting safer. Newly developed security devices enable you to make your castle better-fortified every month. If you ever sell, you'll recapture your investment. Every bit of protection you add keeps you further away from violent conflict and invasion. The average burglary costs you over $1,000, so adding extra protection to your home on a regular basis is a great idea.

ORDER A CHANGING OF THE GUARD (LOCKS)

The first step in securing your home is to change the locks. No matter what your dwelling, a mobile home, an apartment, condo or house, change the locks! Contact a bonded locksmith or just pull your old locks out and visit a hardware store for a replacement. Do this the day you move in. Replace **all** the locks in your home. Most new house builders use cheap locks. For some extra money, you can get a door lock which can't be picked. Police estimate that 25% of apartment burglary comes from managers and building superintendents with a key. If you bought a new house, replace the locks. Ask the builder how many extra keys are floating around. "Well let's see now, the electrician had to have one, the plumber, the floor guy, oh yeah and that fellow who said he was with the exterminator company......" Did the builder get all of the keys back? Sure. . . ! While replacing locks, install security hardware from M.A.G. Engineering of Huntington Beach, CA @ 714-891-5100. They make effective striker plates and latch guards to keep your door from being kicked in.

In addition to installing new locks, install double key, dead bolt locks on outside doors and on the door connecting the garage and house. For convenience, key these locks the same as the door locks.

This is a priority item because it's a defense **against night intrusion**. Most simple burglary happens during the day. If someone breaks into your house at night, they probably want more than possessions. If possible, block the intruder or make entry damn inconvenient. Otherwise, you could be required to take violent action in defense of your home or family.

WHO'S THERE? PROFESSIONAL THIEF OR SICKY?

Professional house burglars are not much of a personal threat; they try to avoid occupied homes. The real pros will often let themselves be caught rather than risk killing or seriously injuring themselves. Therefore, if someone breaks into your house while you're at home, you can assume this is serious—probably deadly—trouble. Nobody can put a handle on what the sick ones will do in your house. The real nut cases may be breaking into your home with the goal of rape or murder. Others may break in on a lark to get money for a drug habit. Even if they have no intention of hurting anyone when they break in, they'll panic when cornered, and this makes them deadlier than a cobra snake. Probably, whoever breaks into your home is prepared to kill you, or do severe bodily harm to get what they want. This is the gravest extreme; be prepared mentally to handle it. Since you can't tell one from the other, consider the situation to be the worst case and act accordingly. Shoot to kill—several times.

IF YOU GO AWAY ON VACATION, ETC.

Try your best to make it look and sound as if someone is home. A device on your lamp line will turn the lights on and off at random times. Leave a radio playing on a talk station. Close some of the blinds so that a burglar hunting for his next victim has to worry about what he can't see. Ask your neighbor to park his car in your driveway during your absence. **Don't** allow mail, flyers, newspapers, etc. to build up in front of your house. If you return to an opened home, never enter. Go to a neighbor and call police.

LIGHT UP THE NIGHT

Install lights. Several retail outlets sell a security light which turns on automatically when something moves in front of its eye. Put these lights on all four sides of your home. These automatic turn-on lights work well also on an RV. You'll probably never know the number of actual peeping toms, burglars and other real intruders the lights turn away.

Another inexpensive item to consider is the two-way, four-station intercom available from Radio Shack. Battery powered, they work equally well in any recreational vehicle, even a tent. With one of the remote speakers mounted near your front door, you don't have to open the door or look through the peephole to see who is there. You can operate this 9-volt battery-powered wonder from the safety of your bedroom sanctuary. If you turn up the volume, you can hear close whispering or a conversation out in the street.

Heavy duty safety chains on all outside doors help, but anybody for whom you open the door just a crack can cut most chains in seconds with a small bolt cutter. The newer models are made with case-hardened steel chain but even if the chain holds, the screws may not. Long, stainless steel screws are best. If you pre-drill the holes, squirt glue into them before you run the screws in.

Never open a door to see who's there! Install peep holes in all solid outside doors, but watch your lighting. If you're back-lighted inside and someone is standing outside in the dark, they can see in nearly as well as you normally see out. After dark, make sure you turn off the inside light and turn on the outside porch light before you approach the door. That way, you can see out the peep hole but anyone standing outside can't see in.

Next, replace all the window latches. Builders who use cheap door hardware use cheaper window latches. Good locks, strong latches and hinges are the cheapest insurance you can buy. Sad to say, though, you can't depend on strong locks alone.

Once your locks and latches are replaced, you've eliminated a good percentage of burglaries. For even more security in your home, you have to do something about the windows. Various grades of shatter resistant glass are available, but they're expensive and none withstand repeated blows from a heavy hammer or crow bar. To secure the glass, install attractive decorative window and door grill work such as you see in Mexico and South America. When you install these units, make sure you can release them from inside in the event of fire.

Don't think you've won the war after you install grills. Criminals have taught me how to go fishin'. With a pole and a hook, you can reach in through the bars on any open window and snag a purse, wallet, **keys,** or anything else within eight feet. Besides the fishing pole technique, the same people teach little kids how to unlock doors from the inside. They slip the child through the window bars, and then walk in through an opened door.

If you don't like grills, try storm windows. They add to the security of your home and also reduce the cost of heating and cooling by as much as 25%. Also, **Maxwell Alarm Screens** work well. We tested these. You can leave your screened windows open all day or night and still be protected. Internal movement, light or sound won't set these off; it takes tampering from the outside. You can get these for windows or sliding doors. Call 800-4-SCREEN for more information.

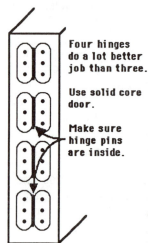

Four hinges do a lot better job than three.

Use solid core door.

Make sure hinge pins are inside.

Install solid wood or insulated metal doors rather than hollow-core junk. When you install solid-core doors, ask the door builder to rout in another cut for an extra hinge or two. Naturally, you must have all your hinge pins accessible <u>only</u> from the inside. When you install your hinges, drill deep into the door and use screws—extra long and strong. Don't buy glass insets for exterior doors; they invite burglars.

Avoid sliding glass doors. They provide easy access routes into your home and are difficult to secure. Where these doors are already in place build a grill to cover the entire unit. At least install a drop stick to keep them from being forced open from the outside. Better, buy two or more locking gadgets. Then put sensors on them when you install your Transcience electronic break-in detection system. We installed one of these in our home office; it was inexpensive and provides terrific security.

Purchase a cheap revolving yellow light for the roof of your house, and remote switch this to the inside of your sanctuary. If you call the police, flip the switch; it will save them from having to look for a house number. Tell the police dispatcher your revolving yellow light is on; that message will go out over the radio. Another way: use a special switch for porch or street number lights. Flip it once to turn them on. Flip twice to make them blink.

USING ANIMALS FOR PROTECTION

Even before you install good locks, bright lights and grill work, get a dog. Any dog! Big, mean-looking dogs are great, but little, loud, nasty dogs are good too. Dogs not only make your home less attractive to burglars, they're also great for letting you know if there is some other life-threatening problem. They smell smoke well before most electronic smoke detectors do, and they sense big storms long before arrival.

Dogs can be neutralized in a number of ways. But the time it takes for an assailant to deal with your dog may give you the precious time in which you escape or shoot.

Defensive dogs come in two varieties, attack dogs and guard dogs. You can teach a dog to attack on command. To get that kind of dog trained up, you normally need to spend between $500 and $1,000 with a trainer. When the dog is about 6 months old, a trainer will teach obedience, and then offensive tactics. Though the idea may be appealing, that's not what you need.

The second variety of dog guards your house or vehicle. They also need obedience school, and you should take them yourself. The more time you spend with your dog, the more the dog will be devoted to you. When the dog is still young, it's a good idea to pay strangers to invade his territory and run away when he barks and charges. Praise it up lavishly after it attempts to protect your territory. Pretty soon the dog gets the idea to protect your yard, your house, and your car anytime you ask.

WHAT BREED?

Unless you have a great deal of time and money to spend, I don't recommend the traditional guard dogs for the sole purpose of home defense. Mixed breeds cost less and have a tendency to be more physically stable than many of the larger registered canines. The mixed breeds I've known have displayed admirable levels of determination and a willingness to do battle. At the same time, these dogs have been the best-natured toward family and friends.

A trained dog becomes a valuable and integral part of your home defense system. This will be hard to do, but keep the dog at an emotional distance. If trouble occurs, never put yourself at risk to try to save the dog. In most cases the dog is better equipped to defend himself than you are. You might also confuse the dog or get in its way, thereby limiting its ability to defend itself.

SIGNS FOR SECURITY

Any or all of these signs might help:

BEWARE OF DOG.   Even if you don't have a dog a sign can be a real deterrent. HOME PROTECTED BY "SUPERIOR ALARM CO." "QUIET PLEASE. DAY SLEEPER" announces someone is at home all day. "PROPERTY UNDER VIDEO SURVEILLANCE" tells a burglar to smile; he's on candid camera. Any smile can and will be used against him in a court of law. Two other signs we like: "DO YOU BELIEVE IN LIFE AFTER DEATH?" TRESPASS IN THIS HOUSE AND FIND OUT FOR SURE. Finally, "THIS HOME IS PROTECTED BY SHOTGUN THREE NIGHTS A WEEK, YOU GUESS WHICH THREE."

CHAIN LINK FENCING

Chain-link fence (6 ft.) and gates at the driveway are a great security addition to any property. That's why our government installs so much chain-link fence. Nothing is better. Set the posts deep into concrete. A single strand of electric fencing on top can be shocking.

Don't use solid wood or brick wall fencing. These give thieves and other outlaws the kind of privacy they crave. Five-foot-high, split rail fencing backed with 2x4 mesh "horse wire" makes a sturdy, attractive, hard-to-climb fence. A single strand of barbed wire wrapped loosely around the top rail of such a fence increases security effectiveness. Don't set anything outside your fence which would make the fence easy to climb.

DRIVEWAY SECURITY

PILLARS FROM BRICK AND A LOCKING GATE

EVEN WITHOUT FENCING

For your driveway, attractive stone or brick pillars allow you to hang lockable gates. This deprives thieves of vehicle access to your possessions. They don't like to carry heavy TV's across the yard to a vehicle. (If they weren't so lazy they might not be thieves.) Besides that, they don't want to be seen.

Invest in a safe deposit box at your local bank. Keep all your expensive jewelry, negotiable bonds, insurance papers, rare coins and other highly portable and disposable valuables in the box. Let anyone who asks about your valuables know you don't keep them in your home. Where you do keep them is nobody's business.

Make an inventory of your possessions. Estimate what it would cost to replace them or insure them for full value. Most people are surprised to find just how much in value they've accumulated. Unfortunately, most people don't discover this until they're filling out insurance claims.

YOUR VAULT
Build your own security room or vault. The best locations are in a corner of your house——on either the second floor or in the basement. A basement corner where the walls are back-filled on the outside is the most secure and the easiest conversion. Once built, it will be a strong, hard-to-violate security locker.

Use 2 x 6 studs. Drill the studs for electric wiring at knee height. At waist height and perhaps other places, drill the studs and set rebar in through the holes. Cover both sides of the walls with diagonal 2 X 6. (If you use surplus lumber, treat for insects.) Next, solid sheet both sides with heavy duty plywood. Glue that plywood to the diagonal 2 X 6 with panel adhesive and nail

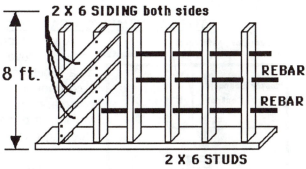

BUILDING YOUR OWN HOME VAULT

2 X 6 SIDING both sides

8 ft.

REBAR

REBAR

2 X 6 STUDS

it on with screw nails. Panel or paint the inside. Hang a steel insert or solid core door only an archangel with Tomb of Jesus experience could penetrate. On four hinges, hang the door so the hinge pins are inside. This makes it nearly impossible for someone to force the door open or to tear it away from the frame. Put two (same key) dead bolts on it, one located a foot from the top of the door and the other located a foot and a half from the bottom. Use battery operated lights.

You can build your vault for less than the cost of a home safe. At the same time, you get five to ten times the secure storage space. Steel gun safes are still a worthwhile investment for storing cameras, silver, jewelry and firearms. For double protection, put your gun safe into your home-built security vault.

DECOY FOR A THIEF
National crime figures tell us the professional thief stays less than five minutes in a home. To save the farm, all you have to do is make it unprofitable after five minutes of collecting. Leave a decoy; once he thinks he's scored, he's out of there. Attend a business auction and buy an old safe. Hide it where a thief can discover it easily, and store some precious junk and fakes in it. Perhaps you'll include a few pieces of costume jewelry, a stack of stock certificates from defunct companies, a sack of small coins.

MARKING YOUR POSSESSIONS
Inventory everything in your home and take pictures. Record every item's serial number and put your name on everything else. This will help you when dealing with your insurance company. Your social security number on your possessions will also help the recovering agency to find you. If you can't prove ownership of stolen property, the perp often goes free and you don't get your stuff back.

THE SANCTUARY OR, SAFE ROOM

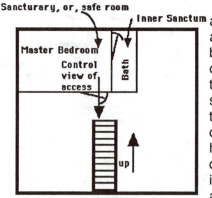

Sancturary, or, safe room
Inner Sanctum
Master Bedroom
Control view of access
Bath
up

Any room providing you with an additional level of security serves as a sanctuary in your home. The best choice is a bedroom with a commanding view of the head of the stairs or the hall separating sleeping quarters from the rest of the home. Most often, that's your own master bedroom. Usually, it has a phone and a bathroom you can use as an inner sanctum with its own a source of water and first aid gear.

Install solid core doors with dead bolt locks to make these areas secure. A cross bolt drop-in 2 X 4 makes the doors battering ram proof.

Children often become aware of danger on their own. Therefore, teach them to go to the sanctuary when they think they're in danger. Be sure to acquaint your baby sitters with the sanctuary concept and defense procedures you want them to use. Pay special attention to window security in your sanctuary. On the ground floor, or if easily reached from any place on the roof, install stout grills on sanctuary windows. Again, **Maxwell Alarm Screens** are a good idea. For windows two stories high with no outside access, include a chain or rope ladder so you can escape.

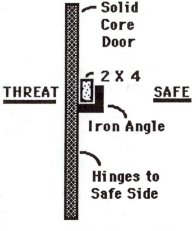

Take into account exceptional circumstances. Is there a handicapped member in your family? Maybe you'll use that person's room for a sanctuary or move the person to your master bedroom.

Our favorite home alarm system is called the Supervisor, from Transcience (**1-800-243-3494**). At #1, the alarm senses motion from an intruder which you turn off with a secret 4 digit number on your control keypad. If not disarmed, then #2, the alarm control, calls the monitoring station, #3, which in turn calls the house to verify or calls police right away.

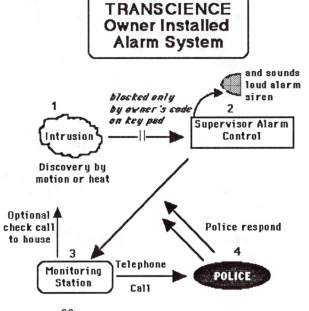

29

We installed one of these systems ourselves and the thing works beautifully. As an added $150 option, you can have it sense smoke and call the fire department. We also added a panic button. The whole alarm system starts for around $600. You save on installation by doing it yourself. After the company receives your floor plan, they tell you exactly where to locate and install everything. Afterwards, you get the feeling you're living in a well-guarded fortress.

Don't keep all valuables in your sanctuary. You don't want to draw a threat to that area. Instead, you want to be able to use the wealth stored elsewhere in your home as a bargaining chip to gain time while you either wait for help or start shooting.

Make this announcement: "Listen carefully; there is nothing of value stored in this area of the house. There is a safe downstairs, and the combination is 36-12-25. Take what you want and leave. If you come towards this area, **we** will kill you." Never let on to someone who has broken into your home that you're alone. Examples: "We," not "I" and, "Our," not "My."

In addition to your self defense weapons, store two top quality flashlights with extra bulbs and batteries in your sanctuary. If you have a portable cellular phone, keep that in the sanctuary with you, too.

Except defense firearms, store weapons in your vault room or gun safe. Store bolt action rifles with the bolts removed and semi-automatic pistols with the slides removed from the frames. Ammo is stored separately. Put the bolts and slides in a separate locking storage box. Therefore, the weapons can't readily be used against you and half a weapon is just so much scrap metal, both to the fence and the thief. Also, nobody will use it on a future victim.

THE INNER SANCTUM

Within your sanctuary, you need a special place where your children and others can wait out the event. With an extra layer of protection between them and danger, they'll be out of harm's way. Nobody comes out of the Inner Sanctum until you give them a pre-arranged signal. If you get into trouble, they'll have to tough it out until help arrives. Either a large walk-in closet or a bathroom will suffice. Just as with your sanctuary, pay special attention to the door and window.

SECONDARY SAFE ROOM

In a large home or one with several floors it's a good idea to establish a second safe room close to where you spend most of your time. Set the second safe room up like the first. You'll want extra insulation between you and a threat, a strong door and good lock, and a defense weapon secure and well hidden, but loaded and handy. Put a phone in this room also.

WORKMEN IN YOUR HOME

Of course, don't hire some bum with a sign that says, "WILL WORK FOR FOOD." The scam often goes like this: "I'm really a willing worker. Just let me come to your house; I can fix anything." Then later, he comes back and steals everything in sight. If he gets caught, he says, "They hired me and didn't pay me." Even if the explanation doesn't work and he goes to jail, he's gotten what he wanted.

When real workers come to install or fix anything, keep your valuables out of sight. Stay at home while the installation is being made and keep an eye on the crew. Find out how long they have been with the company. Before you decide on a company, find out if its bond covers the installation and service personnel against theft. One more note on employees in your home: Choose baby sitters carefully; don't use strangers.

APARTMENT SECURITY

Apartment dwellers may face different problems. Ideally an apartment house would have enclosed parking with limited access and TV monitoring of the parking area, the entrance and hallways. The next best thing is to have outside doors that lock automatically. Do away with electric latch systems that allow lazy neighbors to unlock the main door without bothering to see who is there. Convicted rapists, child abductors and burglars have explained: They like those buildings because tenants inside feel the false security and often let down their guard. So the perps stand on the entry doorstep with a story and keep on ringing until someone lets them in.

Middle floor apartments are the easiest to secure. With a three story apartment building, the most secure location is a corner unit on the second floor without direct access to a fire escape. If you have a chance to visit your apartment laundry room at night alone, skip it. Lots of crime, especially rape occurs there.

Make sure all doors to the outside or hallway are solid core construction and add the extra hinge. The alarm system is just as viable for apartment dwellers as any other home owner.

WHEN CAN THEY GET YOU?
You're most vulnerable to attack as you leave or arrive at your home or business. Be especially watchful
a. from the time you exit your place of business until you're in your vehicle with doors locked.
b. from the time you exit your vehicle until inside your home.

Be observant, and ready to run or fight, depending on the circumstances. A mistake when you're tired at the end of a long drive can put you in the real estate business in three days. They'll give you a small bit of land, a marble marker, and free advertising--in the obituaries.

YOU'RE AT RISK HERE; IN YOUR OWN GARAGE
We're highly in favor of electric garage door openers, electric gates, or both. Garages are often hiding places for kids who take drugs. Worse, they hide attackers or burglars from street view.

Put a bright bulb in your garage opener. You want to flood the garage with light. Don't leave any place in the garage set up so someone could hide in there and wait for you. Put the door down as soon as you park, especially at night.

RIOTS AND NATURAL DISASTERS
In the face of a natural disaster, or if your neighborhood is embroiled in a civil disturbance, are you going to evacuate or stay and fight? In Florida, Hurricane Andrew demolished Homestead. Even before the winds quit, looters were taking advantage of their neighbors, just hit by disaster, and stealing the last of all they had.

If your strategy will be to leave in the event of disaster or riot, make sure your escape vehicle's tank never drops below half. Keep some extra gas in a safe storage area. Use that fuel and then replace it again every six months or so.

Have a grab-and-run bag packed for each family member and a family weekender bag packed with extra clothing, food and first aid gear. Pack the bag with a defense weapon, ammo, knives, and some form of currency.

At the first sign of trouble get out. Don't wait until the rioters are on your block to move. If you have a second home or a family member or friend you can stay with until order is restored, great. If not, see if Motel Six left a light on for you. Get at least 25 miles away. Notify your entire family and police about your departure.

If you have time before you leave, secure all your valuables in your vault room. No vault room? Put your goodies in your bathrooms, push the lock button on the inside and close the door. Turn on a battery powered radio in that room to a talk station. Leave your TV on. Do the most you can to make looters think someone's home.

A friend of mine from Central Los Angeles plans to put an old TV in the middle of the front yard, break a window pane out of the front door before he departs and spread some old clothes on the front porch and steps. That's to make looters think the house has already been looted. It might work. Publishing the plan in this book won't give away the secret either---because most looters don't read.

You may decide to stay and protect your home. Modify your home defense plan accordingly. Accumulate more weapons, at least one firearm for every adult member of the household. You will also want generous supplies of ammunition and emergency food and drinking water, a complete first aid kit, a small generator and fuel for same, plus several fire extinguishers. Don't forget---prayer helps.

Carefully choose three or four neighbors whom you trust and form a co-op defense force. You're always much better off to form a team. (See Path Finder's *Everybody's Outdoor Survival Guide.* Use coupons in rear of this book to order.)

Set up a neighborhood watch schedule during troubled times. If you can, include a couple of retired members or maybe someone who works a regular night shift and is at home during the day. When the lid blows, it's far easier for a group to defend several homes than it is for individuals to guard each home separately. You will need a communications system linking all members of your defense group. Also, establish a chain of command.

As you continue to implement these instructions, you'll be safer. Work on security; keep making your home safer. Most alarm systems sell improvements you can make later when you have the cash and time to add them on. Transcience, for example, sells door sensors and panic buttons to make their system even better.

The money you spend on various projects to keep you and your family safe from tragedy is the best investment you can make. But it's difficult to comprehend the benefit you gain when you never become a victim. Perhaps you'll appreciate the money you invest when a crime occurs down the street to a friend who didn't make his or her home as secure as you did.

OVERSEAS PRISONS—A CHEAP DETERRENT

Where does it say that after committing a crime, the US owes a criminal a free ride in a prison in American territory? Prisons are overcrowded; early releases are flooding society with human sewage before treatment.

Bond issues for prisons spend taxes in advance which may be needed for future problems such as natural disasters, failure of government-insured businesses like savings and loans, or a war.

Solution: contract with foreign governments in Third World countries to take care of our prisoners on a lease basis. Lease facilities in South Korea or Mexico, for a fraction of the cost. Problems with visitation? Establish a tele-communications network.

Chapter 3

NON-SHOOTING WEAPONS

Today, the idea is to avoid conflict if you can, but to make sure you don't lose any fights you can't avoid. **In criminal conflict, any weapon is better than no weapon.**

Weapons, however don't make you invincible. They just help. By definition, a weapon is only an extension of your fighting ability. If you arm yourself with a twenty-pound baseball bat, (beyond your fighting ability), some gorilla will simply take it away from you. Also, don't face up to a firearm with a stick. When the germs have a gun, just about any weapon you choose could cause you to finish in second place. Understand also, that if you use a firearm in the face of a threat not considered lethal, you could face prosecution. In lower class neighborhoods where crime abounds, social pressure on police and prosecutors to go lightly on criminals is extreme.

Weapons other than firearms definitely have a place in your defense structure. In some areas, it's not legally practical to carry a gun. Even if you shoot in unquestionable, absolute self defense, you would still be guilty of a crime. Besides, you might not have a handgun with you when the need arises, so knowing how to defend yourself with something other than a firearm is a good idea.

35

Let's consider your options. To do that, first understand the elements of combat.   Before you choose a weapon, consider **range, speed, power, control, target accuracy, and operational convenience.** Apply these elements to your own strength and ability.

Range. This term defines the distance to a given target. If you keep an opponent away from you, but still close enough for you to reach out and smack with feeling, you win. Examples: Your legs are longer than his arms so you can kick; your sword or spear is longer than his knife; your Bo (five-foot hardwood shaft) will reach out better than a short club. In this chapter, we'll be discussing long range and short range weapons. The longer the range, the safer you'll be. You risk personal injury any time you get in close to an assailant.

Speed. Quickness counts a lot. If you can move faster than your opponent, you'll score and do some damage before he does. So, a weapon enabling you to strike fast is a good idea. For example, you can jab as you would with a pool cue quickly with your Bo, so the blow lands before a block can deflect it. Note also, you have to be fast enough to get your Bo back out of there before he can grab. Don't choose a weapon you can't control. Lose your weapon in a fight and your assailant gains the advantage you thought you had, but lost.

Power. You have to deliver sufficient force with a blow to make your influence felt. A severe bruise or opened blood vessel generally means you've done damage (as opposed to only pain).   On the other hand, minor bruise or pain merely gets your opponent's adrenaline flowing. Besides that, most criminals anger easily.

Target accuracy. All assailants have delicate target areas. Smacking hard on his shoulder won't help you much. The same force to the throat or groin helps him to see things your way. Some weapons are easier to direct accurately on a desired body target than others. The target body consists of pain producing points, damage producing points, and fatal areas. Take your pick.

Operational convenience. Does it take two hands or one to make your weapon work for you? Can you make it readily available or do you have to unpack and unfold it? How much muscle do you need to cause this weapon to work righteously on your criminal target? If only one hand is required, can you use a separate weapon in the other?

Now, let's examine several options in the light of combat principles. Take a personal inventory. Whether you're tall and strong or short and weak, some kinds of weapons will work best for you. You can either make one or purchase one.

CHAPTER 4

FIREARMS FOR PERSONAL DEFENSE

In our opinion, the current rise in crime is only the tip of the iceberg; we're going to see a lot more.   Criminals see themselves as free to do anything they want. In reality, however, a low self image keeps a man imprisoned to the fear of peer disapproval. In their subculture, rebels are heroes; law abiders are chicken losers.

What if a criminal gets caught? Our criminal justice system protects and aids criminals. One example: On *Larry King Live* (20 Oct 92), LA Police Sgt Stacey Koon said, "Rodney King is above the law, literally." Another: mass releases from prisons as urged by the ACLU due to overcrowding. Today's violent criminal is armed. Often, his weapons are far superior to what police carry.   If you want to survive, you'll have to learn to be your own bodyguard.

FELONY CONVICTION = LOSS OF WELFARE
Would the crime rate go down if criminals knew they would lose welfare? Conviction should cancel all entitlements.

How good a bodyguard can you be? You can study edged weapons and become a master of martial arts. You can carry all kinds of whistles and alarms. But in the streets, only one defensive weapon outranks and outperforms all others---that's a firearm.

Don't buy a gun if you won't train with it; lack of training makes a gun a personal liability rather than an asset. Finally, if you don't secure your home, some burglar will steal your gun and trade it for drugs.

Follow these rules:

1. Never pick up a gun and fake it. It shouldn't be in your hand unless you mean business. Lots of people suffer in prisons because the gun went off accidentally during an argument.

2. Do everything you can to avoid serious problems. Never expose yourself to danger. Take no risks. Let the dog bite, the alarm go off, or the tear gas spray before you shoot. This is a weapon of last resort, and you need to define your own personal limit of abuse before you go to this severe a defense measure.

3. Have **nothing** to do with alcohol or drugs in the same place where guns are kept.

4. Make sure you shoot in self defense. Even though you know you were right, follow all the precautions we lay out in Chapter 11, called, <u>After the Attack.</u>

If you agree to follow the rules above, disregard the gun control sentiment in this country and acquire a firearm. Learn to use it, carry it with you everywhere, learn to maintain it, and practice regularly. Otherwise, you may as well put your name in early to get a reservation on somebody's victim list.

GUN? WHAT KIND?

The options are practically unlimited. Guns are available in every size, shape and finish you can imagine. You can choose from pump, semi-auto, or double barrel shotguns. Pistols come in small, medium or large size. Guns can be blued, nickel plated or stainless steel. In addition to all the finishes, steels, barrel lengths and sizes, you have to tackle the major problem, namely, which caliber (bullet size and bang) to choose.

HANDGUNS

Lower power handguns don't provide sufficient power to insur clean kills, even with multiple hits. The high power offerings are harde to control, (some slap your hand pretty hard,) make a quick second sho more difficult, and pose potential danger when they punch through wall on their way to the next city block.

g
rd

to install $180 dollars worth of laser red dot. These sights help make sure you stay on target as you squeeze the trigger. Also, here's a great way to go at greatly reduced expense: Purchase a squeeze bottle of glow-in-the-dark paste and put a line down the top of the barrel (on top of the rib) so you can see your line of fire in the dark. Once you line up the barrel with your target, the only misses you have to worry about will be high or low. See *Everybody's Outdoor Survival Guide.*

You get what you pay for.

HOW TO BUY

Of course, we recommend a store specializing in firearms sales. You buy the weapon, wait for whatever time your state requires, and pick up your gun. The serial number is registered so authorities looking to prosecute and attorneys looking to file civil suit on behalf of a wounded crook can trace the gun to you. Do that; you're a good citizen.

Criminals out there do something else. Daytime burglars steal lots of weapons, and they target houses with gun ownership stickers on the windows. The number of weapons stolen is so high that the street market price for $400 handgun is around $100.

Others who have no intention of being criminals buy guns from friends, gun shows, swap meets and pawn shops. No record is made of the purchase because they generally pay in cash. No computer or officials knows who owns that gun, and when it winds up with no fingerprints on it in a dumpster or in a large body of water after having shot someone, the bullet used to kill can't be traced to anything or anyone. See chapter 11 in this book and talk to your attorney prior to any incident you might become involved in.

Pay for all your firearms purchases by check or credit card and write the serial number of the weapon down so you (only you) have a permanent record of the purchase. If you buy from a gun dealer, he'll make sure you follow the proper procedures for firearms purchase in your state. Prior to purchasing a secondhand firearm from an individual, ask your local police contact to run the serial number through NCIC (National Crime Information Computer) to make sure it's not stolen.

Are used guns OK? Generally, yes. It's hard to screw up a revolver. If you buy at a gun show, you'll find several expert gunsmiths easily who know guns well and who will give you an inexpensive opinion.

45

A bare handgun without an easy way to carry it is a burden you'll soon learn to avoid. Get good holsters. Of all the load bearing vests for combat, carrying bags for weapons and accessories, and holsters, we like **Eagle Industries'** products. Mention this book, and get a free catalog. Send a short note to: Eagle, 400 Biltmore, #530h, Fenton, MO. 63026. They have improved holsters to the level of art form. Built for comfort and easy access, they allow you to carry your weapon with you at all times, including those times when you won't be carrying a handbag. Without these holsters, it just isn't practical for you to carry a handgun. Since criminals (much in favor of gun control) like to attack when you're not carrying, and Eagle's holsters allow you to carry almost everywhere, you increase your odds of surviving potential crime attacks dramatically. So---in warm tropical climates, you can use an ankle holster, or perhaps a shoulder holster under your Hawaiian shirt. Eagle makes shoulder holders with vertical, angle and side pulls so you get easy access to your handgun the way you like best. That's what's best about Eagle. The variety of holsters they sell allows you to carry your handgun with you rather than leave it at home or in your vehicle.

On the straps supporting the holster, hang a few extra rounds in a small pouch, and perhaps a good folding Blackjack Mamba knife which you can open with one hand. Buy a gun cleaning kit. Better than one for each caliber, get an all-purpose kit. Also, get some lead remover because practice rounds leave lead deposits.

What you've read so far will probably give you enough information to purchase a pistol. Though we could fill a book (and we did in *Great Livin' in Grubby Times*) let's mention a few others.

Automatic pistols are flatter than revolvers and therefore don't bulge on your body. Think concealment. They also hold more ammo. Many come in a heavier caliber with more stopping power than the .38 Special. But, they're like spouses; they require tender loving care if you want them to be faithful. Otherwise, they can fail when you need them most. Most home defense shooting confrontations are settled with one shot. So you need a weapon that works—every time! You don't generally need a 50 round drum magazine or "the most powerful handgun in the world." You need a weapon you can use effectively under the most stressful circumstances. For all of the above reasons, we vote for revolver. Double action revolvers are safe and sure.

Rim fire cartridges are .22's. Someone on drugs may not feel the pain or be bothered much unless you hit a vital organ because the little bullets don't do a lot of damage. If all you have is a .22, keep on loading lead into your customer 'til the gun is empty. Otherwise, the perp can get back up—-with a temper. You can get a .22 magnum, which does more damage, but still not enough. Since you can't reload a rim fire, you're stuck with the manufacturer's bullet. Penetration through a barricade or even heavy over clothes will be poor. If you shoot through auto glass, especially from an angle, you'll get some bullet deflection.

WHAT SHOULD A CONVICT LOSE?
What about citizenship? Even if all citizenship rights weren't forfeit, what about a loss in civil rights? Once convicted of a crime, we know who they are and what they do, so their right to remain silent after arrest should no longer exist. Technical laws on search and seizure which would toss evidence against them would no longer be invocable. Anything found in their possession should be used against them in prosecution, no matter how obtained. Anything they said to anyone, anywhere, would be the same as foreign military radio transmission---totally free and usable. After all, we are at war, aren't we?

Center fire cartridges smaller than .38 Special are .25, and .32 or .380 (a mini 9 millimeter—-best of the small ones). Unless a .38 Special is too much gun for you, leave the smaller ones in the store.

The main consideration in purchasing a firearm is this:

Buy a gun you can handle.

Don't exceed your limitations, but choose weapons that provide all the power you can manage, as well as all the weight you are able to carry comfortably. Remember, special ammo adds heft to your handgun. We are very impressed with **Lock and Load's** defense ammo offerings. Other good defense loads are available from Remington, Federal and the Winchester Black Talon loads are superb.

The longer the barrel on a pistol, the more accurately it will shoot at a distance. **But,** the easier it will be for somebody close to take it away from you, and the tougher it will be to conceal. Stay under 4 inches.

If you can handle more than a .38 Special, you can go to 9 mm, which shoots a lighter bullet at the speed of a .357 magnum. The 9 mm. handguns hold as many as 19 rounds; that's real fire power.

The .357 magnum shoots the same bullet as the .38 Special—only faster. Make sure you can handle the weight, blast, and recoil before you invest, otherwise your pistol will sit around at home. If you go for a 9 mm., get **Lock and Loads'** (703-289-6892) heavyweights, which leave the muzzle at 1,000 feet per second and release three lead balls as they expand to .55 caliber.

The .41 magnum, in our opinion, is not a practical choice for a home defense weapon. The size, weight, high cost, and lack of choice in ammunition variety are the reasons for our decision.

The .44 magnum jumped in popularity when the gun jumped in *Dirty Harry's* hand. It was billed as the "most powerful handgun in the world." Audiences got a thrill when Harry told the bank robber, "Go ahead...make my day." The recoil of the weapon flying in the air was real. It will smack you. Go ahead, believe what you saw. Believe also the eardrum-busting muzzle blast. Maybe you should pass.

On the other hand, you may already own one, which you find difficult to shoot accurately. If that's the case, try .44 Special ammo. The reduced blast and recoil may be all you need to keep you on target accurately.

Finally, we discuss the famed .45 automatic. It pushes a 230 grain (heavy) projectile out of the barrel at about 850 feet per second (relatively slow) which causes most of the bullet energy to transfer to the target. But the .45 pistol can be tough to shoot accurately unless you're prepared to spend plenty of time and money for practice ammo.

What does Huber use? A .45 automatic with all bells and whistles. The accessories, sighting system and extras he has on his personal pistol make it worth about $1,500. He practices quite a bit, too. Every year he makes it a point to shoot at least 3,000 rounds through his .45. Huber hates lawsuits, and his .45 insures that no post shooting litigation will be filed.

You have a lot to learn with a .45 auto. The model 1911 and subsequent series (for the year they first came out) are still popular today and a lot of them are around, in homes, on firing ranges etc. Unlike more modern designs, they can fire without a magazine inserted, so the weapon is **not clear** just because you remove a full magazine. Also, holding your thumb up behind the slide while firing can cause severe pain and injury. If you're thinking of buying a .45, think again. A hit with a light bullet is far better than a miss with a heavy one. Don't buy too much gun. Make sure you can handle any big caliber before you buy. Remember, you can make a smaller caliber handgun much more effective with custom ammunition.

<u>SHOTGUNS</u>

One well aimed shot from any shotgun will terminate just about any home defense problem. Anybody who has seen the devastation a shotgun can do at close range has developed healthy respect for this weapon. The thought of a loaded shotgun in the hands of a homeowner causes criminals to have nightmares. If I were a burglar and heard the noise of a shell racking into a shotgun's chamber, I'd be concerned, to say the least.

Like handgun calibers, shotgun shells also come large and small—-called gauges. This is tricky because the bigger the number, the smaller the gauge. The quick fix: Ladies get a 20 gauge with a three inch chamber, and men can handle a 12 gauge. The in-between sizes don't make a whole lot of sense. Exception: very small women who are not too athletic can use a .410.

Once you've purchased the correct gauge, think about shot charge. At least it's consistent with gauges; the bigger the number, the smaller the shot. So #2, (.27) shot is bigger than #4, (.24) and #8 shot is a load commonly used for hunting small birds. For defense purposes, at ranges less than 20 yards, a load of #2's or #4's will do just fine. Don't buy steel shot for defense, especially in moist, tropical climates. Long storage periods in damp climates can cause the shot to rust together, which jeopardizes the shotgun when fired. To be ready for longer range shooting, (+50 yards) go to a double-ought buck load, (designated 00-BUCK on the box). In a plastic cup, you get 9 balls, each about a third of an inch in diameter, flying towards your target at 1050 feet per second. That's OK, but what I really like is the spread. Shotguns are also called scatter guns, and the farther away you are from a target, the wider the pattern. Of course, too far away and all the shot may land *around* the target, rather than *on* it. Also, you need to know: the smaller the shot, (bigger number) the less effective it will be at long range. That's why some of us prefer slugs.

You **must** pattern your shotgun. Otherwise, you'll never know where it shoots. Simply shoot carefully at a marked spot on a large cardboard box and see where all the shot goes. You're hoping for an evenly dispersed pattern around your aim point. If you don't get that, either compensate by aiming off or visit your gunsmith.

Shotguns are smoothbore guns, so they get a slug to twist as it flies out of the barrel by putting vanes in the slug. Properly called rifled slugs, these reach out farther than shot loads, and provide enough accuracy to be effective up to 100 yards, where they shoot 8" groups.

If you read **Great Livin' in Grubby Times,** (found at most Army/Navy stores), you'll pass on a handgun and buy a shotgun for survival. They are cheaper and out-perform a pistol by quite a margin. For home defense, shotguns' big advantage is the noise they make---not when shot, but when racked. Anybody in the crime business knows the sound a shotgun makes when a round racks into the chamber. Most bad guys will run like a scared deer. Statistics tell us over 12 burglars flee for every one who fights after hearing a shotgun being prepared for battle. But, shotguns require two hands to shoot and can't be carried around easily. They're cumbersome in tight spaces. If you get a shotgun, folding stocks are a good idea, and laser sighting systems are wonderful for night work. Flashlights give away your position and draw fire. Also, the 12 gauge recoil often breaks flashlight bulbs.

Do you want an automatic, pump or double barrel? Doubles are fine because they are super reliable. Also, most home defense situations are decided with one shot, and your double gives you an extra shot (quick) for reinforcement. Like auto pistols, auto scatterguns become temperamental with no TLC. A light load in an auto shotgun will make it fail to feed. Also, all ammunition doesn't fit in all automatics. If you buy a box of shells which doesn't chamber correctly, the gun can't fire. Pumps require muscle but are more reliable. I vote for the pump. It will be as reliable as your racking arm. Mine is a S&W 3000 with folding stock. The tubular magazine under the barrel holds 7 shells. Like an automatic pistol, this is a LIFO loader. Therefore, I put two slugs in first. (To chamber last). In a close quarter squabble, I'll never fire them. That's because tubular magazines on most shotguns provide you with a wonderful facility, you can reload anytime, anywhere, with zero down time (time when the weapon can't be fired). You just stuff shells into the tube, either while changing position or safe behind a barricade. If I could only have one weapon for home defense, I'd choose my Remington 870.

We leave rifles out of this discussion because they're a long range weapon. Criminals who want to rob and attack you do it from close range.

Citizen in defense
Prima Facia diminished mental capacity.

Statistics prove that the average law-abiding citizen and the criminal come into conflict. The severity of the conflict will be dictated by the experience, will to fight, weaponry and skill of the two combatants.

As a law-abiding citizen, you stand to lose in all three areas. Criminals have more skill because they have more experience in street fighting. With welfare to take care of their needs, they have plenty of time to plan and practice. Citizens have less fighting skill because they have full time jobs and no time to practice defense measures. Criminals have better weaponry because they don't care about laws controlling guns, which citizens obey. Criminals have a tremendous will to fight because they feel no restraint from criminal justice and are often reinforced by drugs. Law-abiders, on the other hand, don't really want to hurt anybody, and are afraid of arrest. Winning could be worse than losing if the justice system later decides the intended victim committed a crime while fighting for survival. Drugs don't make their nature vicious.

Because of these differences in combatants, the law must give defending citizens a special legal status, and presuppose **that victim-defenders operate with a diminished mental capacity.** This presupposition would give winning victims a benefit in trial or sentencing, as well as relieve them from civil liability after a shooting.

Finally, you need to understand something about weapons very few people consider, probably because of the way Hollywood portrays gunfights. There's a definite hierarchy of weapons, and to stay alive, you need to understand it. In most peoples' hands, handguns can't place bullets as accurately or shoot as effectively at long distance.

Pistols are only more effective if you shoot at close range and shoot first. If you plan on using your .38 Special to tangle with a shotgun or rifle, buy life insurance. To survive in any shooting disagreement, this general rule applies:

51

Try to avoid combat with a weapon where you have only a 50% chance of winning. Break off contact, give up your goods, or come back from a different angle with a new weapon. But don't risk your life if you have another option.

As part of that philosophy, never draw your weapon if you're not absolutely sure you can be first. Drawing a pistol in close (grappling range) quarters with your attacker could cause you to lose it. Witness the number of police officers shot with their own gun.

As long as you'll be packing iron around, get a concealed weapons permit for each adult. Call and ask what the requirements are before you appear in person. Many jurisdictions require that you state you were raped or you carry payroll money and feel at risk before they'll issue. To get the permit, you'll have to tell them what they want to hear.

Finally, stay in good physical condition. You'd be surprised at how low you can go. Criminals are looking for weak victims, and you will look weak if you let yourself get out of shape. Aerobic exercise three times a week is best. Add some gym training for muscle tone. If you spend the time to stay in shape, you'll look alert. Having an effective weapon on your person with which you are competent will also give you a confident attitude. Most criminals read that attitude as a "detour-to-some-other-victim" sign.

Combined with regular shooting practice, a healthy physical appearance, and quick access to firepower, your chances of winding up in the news as a victim will be substantially less.

SIXTH SENSE ADMISSIBLE IN COURT

Citizens are not allowed to use more force than that which they perceive as being used on them. When a citizen uses more force, he or she is subject to criminal prosecution. Key word here is "perceive." As it stands, criminal records and malfeasant intent of any criminal is only subject to objective test as perceived by five senses. New law would create a sixth sense available to citizens. If the criminal had previous conviction or previous arrest, then citizen's assessment of danger was correct, and the danger perceived was real. Therefore, no prosecution for too strong a response against invasion or attack.

Chapter 5

TRAINING FOR DEFENSE AGAINST CRIME

Most victims of criminal germs never got ready to fight the battle. They were caught by surprise, didn't know what to do, were too terrified to think, and lost by default.   Those who live through the experience explain their losses with phrases such as, ". . .right out in broad daylight;" or, . . "there was a whole gang of them;" or, "right in my very own yard."   Many of those victimized would have won the battle with only a little preparation and training.

When you increase training, you lessen the chances of losing in criminal conflict.   To be sure, in the event you're faced with a violent situation and you don't have access to a firearm, you can use a handy knife, club or other non-shooting weapon. But you need to practice so you'll be able to strike quickly with power.   Often, you can turn a losing situation into a winning one with nothing more than a primitive weapon.

But don't go up against a firearm with a lesser weapon unless you have no choice. Push come to shove, if I am unarmed and cornered by a thief with a knife, I might try a couple of the moves I've learned along the way. But if the same thug pulls a gun on me while I only have a baseball bat, I'll do nearly anything he tells me to. The instant I feel he's going to shoot, I am not going to just stand there and take it. No matter how poor my chances are, any chance is better than none. What I do will depend on my position relative to his, and the sense I get of his ability. I'll be ready to take advantage of any diversion that might occur. I'll be watching for the smallest opportunity. Finally, I'll be looking for anything I can get my hands on to use as a weapon—-anything. Hopefully, my training and practice will carry the moment.

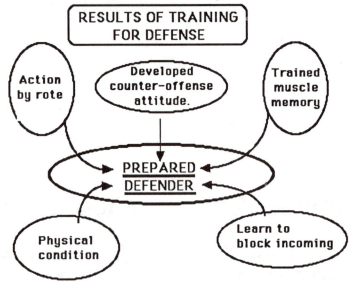

Training does important things for you. First, personal stress in a life-or-death situation can block your ability to think; you won't be able to think at all. Training helps to take you out of that paralysis. Second, to be quick and effective, you need to be able to perform by rote, like a robot. If you don't train, you don't install any habit of action. Third, you have to pre-form a determined attitude of counter offense in order to overcome what the Los Angeles PD calls "lag time." It's normal for most good citizens to be appalled at the prospect of shooting, knifing, or beating someone with a club, but those actions may be required for survival. To succeed in war, you just have to fight better than the enemy. If you have the slightest doubt about the less-than-animal mentality of the modern criminal mind, read a few crime reports.

ATTITUDE TRAINING
Every time you train with a weapon, you re-groove your mental attitude. Don't just stand there hitting a tree or fence post with your Bo. Make pretend this is real—a life or death situation with a drug crazed moron who wants to hurt you. Avoid all the trouble you can. But if you can't avoid the trouble, decide now to give the other side an opportunity to find out firsthand if there really is life after death.

54

In line with keeping your attitude right, learn the concept of focus. Focus intensely on the part of the anatomy you want to influence. As defined by Sun Duk Sun, the 9th degree grand master of Tae Kwon Do, "focus" means you bring all of your strength, heart, mind, soul, and striking force to one point on your opponent's anatomy. That's what you do with the tree limb. Poke with the ends of the limbs as hard and fast as you can. Smooth out the side of the bat to be held by your guiding, or, non-propelling hand. You want the bat to slide back and forth easily.

How does your conscience react to all of this? Let us help you. The anger and hatred the perp exhibits weren't caused by you. You'll feel as if you caused it. But that's because the perpetrator exudes hatred as if it were directed solely at you. But the attitude is his—and always will be. Those hateful sentiments were rooted in this germ long before you encountered him, and will still be there long after. You can rely on that, even though the jerk doesn't think so (which is why he's full of hatred). He never gets a clue that the real problem is in him rather than in the rest of the world.

Therefore, think this way: if you bury this guy now, you save several potential victims down the road the trouble of being bullied, robbed, raped, or beaten. If you strike first, you do society a favor.

If you're going to use a firearm for self defense, do all of your soul searching and moralizing long before the battle with the enemy descends upon you. Then, when it's life or death, make sure it's the other person's death and your life. Shoot to kill and keep on shooting until you are 110% absolutely certain the threat has been neutralized— with extreme prejudice.

To prepare for war, you do two types of training:
a. You train physically with the non-shooting weapon of your choice. Make sure you can strike your target often with precision and strength. Set aside between one to four hours a month where you can work out with the weapon you've chosen. Don't try to become proficient with a Bo, a Tonfa, and your baseball bat. Choose one weapon, and half a dozen moves and strikes. What's the best time to practice with a weapon? After dark. That's when most criminals go to work. Also, you'll be less self conscious.

b. Train with your firearm at least bi-monthly. Don't merely go to a range, stand up sideways, and shoot. Use barricades; shoot and move; practice a lot at night. In the desert or woods, find an old car you can shoot at from various angles so you know how your particular rounds will penetrate. Shoot through wood as well. Caution: Bullet holes don't belong in anyone else's property. Bring your own wood to shooting practice. Don't <u>ever</u> shoot through an old, abandoned building without checking inside first.

The choice of weapons you have in Chapter Three are: DEFENSIVE SPRAY GAS. We give this show two thumbs up! Work with an innocuous bottle of spray so you learn to aim the real thing. Inspect the spray nozzle on your Mace can; then buy a similar spray can of window cleaner. Now, with the window cleaner, close your eyes, feel for the can, and try to spray ahead of you. If I get my wish, you sprayed window cleaner anywhere (perhaps in your own face) but the target. Here's the point: <u>Modify your Mace spray can so you can use the stuff at night.</u> You need both to <u>see</u> the spray direction easily, **and** <u>feel</u> it. Some spray packages are designed to help you spray without seeing the can. Sabre CS gas mixed with red pepper, for example, sprays right out of the leather case.

If the can of Sabre Gas you bought will spray like a paint can, (in any direction unless you aim), it needs some modification. Pick up the can with your spraying hand. Mark the side of the can where your thumb will rest. Cut a piece of plastic off a plastic fork and use one of the super glues to stick it right where your thumb goes. That way, when your thumb is on the bump, you'll spray straight ahead. Place a similar bump on your practice can of window cleaner. Now you can practice with your eyes closed. With a little training, you'll be able to use Mace in the dark. We recommend that you train with your Mace in your weak (left?) hand so you can free up your strong hand with a second weapon. If you spray someone and they keep on coming toward you, you have a reasonable right to be in mortal fear, and therefore, to use more force. Remember, we advised you to spray

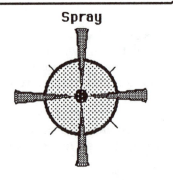

IN WHICH DIRECTION?

Spray

with your weak hand and hold a handgun in your strong one. If you'll use a handgun in your right, practice spraying with your left. Once you know where it aims, spray the cleaner on a mirror or window in which you can see your own image. Spray your own reflection in the face; center on the nose. Make sure you go through the motions with your own can. Get proficient enough to unlock any safety device on your Mace can and spray quickly with only one hand.

KEY CHAINS KEYED TO DEFENSE. Makiwara sticks aren't very useful unless you study karate and learn to snap with them. As a handle for the sinker on your key chain, they're OK because you know they'll always be with you. Use the handle to swing a 2 oz. sinker.

LONG RANGER. The Bo. This is perhaps the best defensive weapon you can use, in this writer's opinion. You can learn to use one by watching a video. Practice on fence posts, trees, and tall shrubs. Naturally, you can pool-cue this a longer distance away. But—-you gotta be quick. (That's why you train.) Otherwise, they'll take it away from you. This weapon works well in the old, rifle-butt-stroke mode. You can also swing it like a bat. If you make your own Bo from a tree limb, leave a hook on one (lower) end so you can hook the legs out from under any attacker before he gets in close.

The Bo is also an excellent blocking tool. With a thick wood center portion, you can drill through and then carve out a hand-hold to protect your knuckles. Tapering the ends makes the Bo lighter; therefore, it will strike faster and harder. With fresh tree hardwood, bake it over an open fire; the heat will harden the wood like iron.

THE TONFA. This side handled baton is nothing to fool with if you haven't learned how and if you don't practice consistently. Learn to swing with one hand while extending the other arm up, out of the way. Draw the swinging hand in close to your chest to prevent breaking a bone of your own. (Trainee police officers in LA. routinely break their own arms.) Another way, use two hands on the handle. This great tool blocks, swings, (both forehand and backhand) hooks, and jabs—-both forward and behind. But you have to learn how; otherwise, you'll be much better off with a Bo.

CUTTING TOOLS. When women use knives for defense, their lag time often gives perps a good chance to take it away from them. That's a severe problem. Don't buy a knife for defense unless you also buy a rubber knife for practice.   The knife maker most prominently into knives as weapons is probably Cold Steel.   The company's owner is a leading authority on edged weapon combat and has gone beyond martial arts. To be good with a knife, you really have to practice a lot.

Here's one important thing to remember:
Don't bring a knife to a gunfight.

OTHER DESPERATION WEAPONS
Grab a thick piece of cloth and break a window, then wrap the cloth around a piece of glass and slice with it. Drop a rock in your sock. Shorten your grip so you swing from the sock's heel. (Otherwise, it may swing around and hit you.) A chunk of concrete in a belt will also do a good job. Military belts are good for this because they cinch all the way up on the concrete. If your belt is leather, punch some extra holes in near the buckle. Practice swinging so the return arc of the swing is not in line with your body.

Incidentally, you can talk defense all you want, but take a lesson from football coaches: The best defense is a good offense. In today's society, offense isn't considered right, so talk "defense," but then know what you're really talking about.   Attack ferociously.

CRITICAL ADVICE: Weapons enable you to take on superior force---if you keep them. Most superior forces try to take them away. Don't strike once and wait around. Retract the weapon as quickly and forcefully as you hit with it.   Then, either strike again or leave.

MARTIAL ARTS
Karate-do means: The way of the empty hand. Weapons training makes you more effective because weapons extend and increase your defense capability. Learning a martial art is good because many martial art moves make your weapons work better, more effectively, faster, and safer (because you learn to strike in balance and not over-extend).

Martial arts training is extremely useful but it may trap you in the beginning, when you begin to feel your own power and think you're now invincible.   Another problem, especially for women, is this: you have to let your attacker come in close (well inside three yards) before you can work your magic.

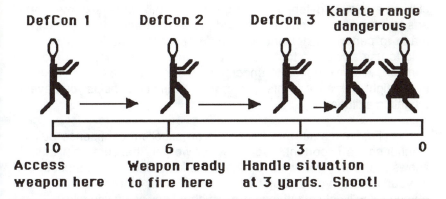

DefCon 1　　　DefCon 2　　　DefCon 3　　Karate range
　　　　　　　　　　　　　　　　　　　　　　dangerous

10　　　　　　　6　　　　　　　3　　　　　　　　0
Access　　　　Weapon ready　Handle situation
weapon here　to fire here　at 3 yards. Shoot!

DEFCON SYSTEM OF PREPARING FOR CONFLICT
The DefCon (Defense Condition) system keeps you from getting caught by surprise because you didn't pay attention to a potential problem early enough. Martial arts training tends to teach you to handle problems inside your three-yard limit. You're better off to address the problem at six yards.

But you should be attacking long before the germ gets that close. Also, the kind of martial arts most women choose to study is karate. It doesn't work well on a grappler, which is what most rapists and women abusers are. Once they grapple with you, they're too close to kick and the contest is often decided by pure strength and size.

CLOSE RANGE COMBAT WHERE STRENGTH AND SIZE PLAY A BIG PART IN CONTEST

Grappling Range
Too close for Karate

Still, martial arts training offers multiple benefits. Any martial art will get you into better than average physical condition,

Most criminals are grapplers when they fight. When they get in too close to you like this, karate doesn't work as well as judo, jujitsu, or aikido.

which will lessen your chances of failing in other areas of defense. It will also increase your chances of winning in violent confrontations if your gun isn't with you. Knowing one or two thoroughly effective and disabling moves really well can make the difference between winning or dying. In a case where using a firearm creates an unacceptable level of risk to people you're trying to protect, having the ability, courage and confidence to attack without a firearm is a good idea. To use a knife or

59

club as a primary defense weapon, you <u>must</u> take at least some martial arts training. If you don't understand the ways in which the body can be made to perform faster and with more applied strength, you won't be able to use a weapon to its fullest advantage or you may lose it during combat. Also, you need to understand blocking and parrying, because in any fight, someone wants to hurt you. Martial arts helps you develop a fighting attitude.

Finally martial arts training is an excellent confidence builder. Confidence is important, especially for women, because that attitude shows in the way you walk (upright, shoulders back, with purpose) and in your tone of voice. Don't worry about what kind of martial art to pursue. You'll get <u>something</u> from just about any study you take.

Your idea may be to take only one short lesson in how to come out a winner in hand-to-hand combat. But, karate instructors have spent years studying their own disciplines. (That's the only way to get a black belt in anything.) If you go to any martial arts class, you'll be studying their martial art. Just make sure the class has one vital element: sparring. Listen to Bruce Lee in a line from *Enter the Dragon.* He says, "Boards do not hit back." If you don't get a chance to face off with other opponents and spar (no contact is required), you aren't training for combat; you're just learning motions to punch holes in the air.

Get a physical checkup if you have any doubts about your condition. Martial arts training can be very strenuous activity. So is active fighting during an attack.

When all is said and done, you need to know what the limitations of your karate ability are. Even if you have a sixth degree black belt, be aware of two things: A. Mental preparation is important; it goes hand in hand with physical ability. You simply have to be ready to attack savagely. A good "street fighter" who is ready and willing to do battle can overcome any karate expert who is not mentally set. B. Firearms are king. The only time a firearm loses to a club or clever karate move is in the movies. If someone else has the firearm and you have a black belt and a Bo, back down, run away, or give up your wallet. Nobody's tougher than a bullet.

FIREARMS TRAINING
As a beginner, you can't learn how to shoot well from a book or video. You really need hands-on training. Call the National Rifle

Association and find out where classes are held near you. You have so many things to learn in the beginning that you can't keep your mind on it all. An instructor will help make sure you stay safer than you could on your own; also you need a trained shooter to watch as you actually shoot, analyze your shot groups, and correct any errors you make shooting or reloading.

You must learn the basics of firearms marksmanship before you can start to develop defensive shooting capabilities. In basics, for example, you learn how the weapon works without firing. You learn to align the sights of the handgun, and how to make those *aligned* sights stay on target. Examples of defensive combat shooting techniques are speed reloading, quick removal from holsters, and shooting from behind barricades. Trying any of these before you learn the basics could be dangerous, and danger around loaded guns can be life changing.

Rifle shooting has often been compared to riding a bike. Even after several years, you can ride. You may wobble a little for the first few minutes, but then you feel as if you never stopped riding. Shooting a handgun well requires constant practice. Keep training and practicing? It's because you can't be wobbling around with your handgun in the first few seconds of a confrontation. That's how you miss and finish second in a field of two. In a high percentage of encounters with a criminal, one shot settles the question of who keeps on breathing. To be smooth and effective with your first round requires constant training and practice. Even if you can't get to the range, dry fire at the guys on your TV screen. Just watch your sights. Learn to focus (in the martial art sense of the word) on the front blade.

How should you practice? As the story goes, G. Gordon Liddy was asked to address a Florida audience on the subject of gun control. After a lengthy introduction, he stood up and said, "Good gun control— is when you use both hands." Then he left. That's what you strive for--- good gun control.

Most people practice by going to a range and calmly firing at paper targets. They practice speed loading and shoot from different distances. The ranges are open from 9:00 A.M. to 5:00 P.M. They practice diligently and use ear protection. The LAPD (PD=Police Dept). recommends shooting 1,000 rounds a year. Do that. You can make a hobby out of it and win trophies. But take note of this if you do what most do: You'll shoot during the daylight hours----outdoors.

61

Finally, you'll think you're ready. You and your handgun have become good friends and you understand each other. You followed our advice on custom loading so your revolver contains the right bullet mix.

Have you noticed this, however? One good crime deterrent is night lighting. Why? Because most criminals have a neurosis about being in light. Guess what? You may be as good as the Lone Ranger in daylight outdoors with your Mickey-Mouse ears on, but your most likely criminal encounter will take place in the dark indoors where gun noise is explosive. You'll not only be exposed to your own muzzle flashes, but perhaps to someone else's.

Of course you'll be scared. It's dark. You can't see your sights, and maybe you never practiced shooting instinctively. The muzzle flash of a pistol in the dark will scare you severely, and if you look at it, your night vision will disappear, causing some people to panic because they think they went blind at the critical moment. The indoor bang will jar you out of your wits. Really, it's amazing.

Now, given this drastic change in shooting conditions, change the way you practice. **Learn how to shoot at night.** You have to shoot indoors a couple of times without hearing protection. Learn not to look directly at your muzzle flash. Nighttime aiming techniques are different. The distance between you and your target will probably be much closer than you ever thought about.

"I determined the maximum practical range for my own home defense practice by measuring the longest distance I can see, point to point, in my own home. Thirty two feet. I then added ten feet to this range. An even fourteen yards. I practice at ranges from five feet out to my maximum. I've resolved not to let a potential threat get closer than five feet as this could neutralize my ability to react." Huber

Of course, you have to develop speed. When bullets are flying around, he who hesitates quits breathing shortly thereafter. Many people think of the speed concept as being fast on the draw. That's not true. It's being first on the draw. As soon as you even get a whiff of possible trouble, your hand should be in your bag, under your coat, or behind your back grabbing your firepower. If you draw the weapon completely out, perhaps use a rag, towel, or handkerchief to cover it while it's ready to shoot.

Ready. Now, watch and listen carefully. If the trouble really develops, shoot first. Timing and accuracy go hand and hand in defensive shooting. Remember the old *Gunsmoke* TV series? The bad guy beat Matt Dillon to the draw at the beginning of those shows, but he missed, Matt didn't. It won't do you one tiny bit of good to fire fast and miss. Never shoot so fast you only punch holes in the air.

The purpose of shooting at a target is to hit. That's the opposite of miss. To hit your target, consider how not to miss. Misses break down into two categories: You either miss off to one side (right/left) or you miss high/low. All you have to do is correct and eliminate the misses and every shot you fire will be a hit.

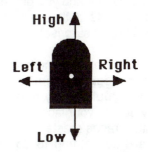

First, let's deal with left/right. Any good pistol shooter knows the method employed for marksmanship. Part of that is: *Align the sights (barrel) with the target, and then squeeze the trigger slowly so that you don't cause the barrel to mis-align.* Think of it this way: it's like taking a picture. Just as you can't move the camera when you shoot, you can't move the weapon when you fire. Assuming that you modified your barrel with Tulip paste, you have a straight phosphorescent line you can point at your target. After that, all you have to do is make sure not to move the weapon left or right when you squeeze the trigger.

Eliminate high and low misses by holding the barrel level. It takes practice. I've see gunfights won by a fast first shot which hit the ground and sprayed pieces of asphalt and bullet fragments all over the adversary's lower body. Those mini-hits distracted him considerably, and bought time for a well-aimed second shot which won the contest, hands down. Naturally, you need a hard surface under you to make this work. But a round on the ground marks the shot so you can check for left right accuracy, **and** insures that your barrel is in line with the target. For this reason, I prefer to shoot low. Shooting high is a natural tendency for all handgun shooters, and confuses the shooter because he has no idea how he missed. Therefore, he can't adjust aim on his second round.

Whenever you practice, count shots forwards. Continue to count; when the word "six" comes out of your mouth, you'd better reload. Don't forget. Train yourself to know at all times how much ammo you've expended. When you get to heaven, you're going to meet a lot of people who got there early in life because they forgot to count. Really--- this is a critical skill in handgun shooting. In a bullet exchange, you're highly at risk as soon as your weapon goes "down" that is, empties. To stay alive, you need to minimize down time, the time your weapon is un-loaded. The key to reloading quickly isn't in how fast you can do it, or what fancy gadgets you use. The key to speedy reloading is preparation, and you get ready with your loading hand on time when you count shots. Otherwise, you shoot away and come up empty as a rather unpleasant surprise.

Here's something else critcal to know: **Don't reload only when your weapon empties. Reload when you have an opportunity, when your enemy least suspects it, or any time you get the urge!** Overcome your lack of training in this area. At the range, during the day, with a range master in charge, you'll empty your pistol, then reload. But that has nothing to do with combat, and it's a dangerous habit to develop. Almost all handgun shooters do the same thing everywhere--- fire until the weapon is empty---and then reload. In a prolonged gunfight, that procedure could get you killed.

With handguns in defense, don't just think about shooting. Think also about getting shot at. The police think about it; that's why so many wear vests. Who might be shooting at you? Will they be any good? When I read H. Norman Schwartzkopf's, *It Doesn't Take a Hero,* I learned how he conducted training---in order to win over the best. That's what you have to do as well. Consider that the criminal you go up against is cunning, street wise, battle-hardened, and ruthless. Let me tell you something about those kinds of guys; they often identify the weapon shooting at them and count shots. It's a good idea; almost everybody shoots and reloads in the Mother Goose mode---Empty-Dumpty. Not you, though. You want to pray that the guy against you is counting, then eject and load again after three. Fire three more and aim the fourth carefully. If he counts---he'll look---just about the time you enter your fourth round into the contest.

Of course, you count, both his and yours. Counting forward is also advantageous for mix 'n match shooters who need to know which round is up. For you, that's important because we want you to practice with cheap ammo and keep hot loads in the weapon ready for the real thing. Therefore, you'll mix 'n match out of several **Lock and Load** packages. Each round has a specific purpose. Two will be expanding shot shells. At a long distance, or to penetrate a barricade, you'll need a Cor-Bon™ round, so shoot the other bullets which won't perform the specific task you need now.

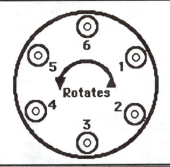

FIRING ORDER FOR MY RUGER SIX SHOT

With any handgun, mix 'n match every magazine or cylinder full of ammo the same. Thus, you can count forward and

Load with 1 Expanding shot; 2, a hollow point. Thumb past 3. Then shoot 4, a .357 magnum blaster to penetrate a barricade.

know exactly what round does what job of penetration, expansion, or long-distance placement. Say you want to shoot a custom bullet on the fourth shot. Magazines are simple to set up; they are LIFO loaders, (Last In, First Out) so you load three more after your custom round. Revolvers can be easy too; you set up the speed loader in the order you would like. But then---you have to match the speed loader to the revolver's cylinder. So you mark them both and line the marks up. Use tulip paste on your cylinder at number five, and mark you speed loader the same way. Even in the dark, you'll get a match, and the first round you fire will be number one.

TARGET RESULT

SIGHTS DISTURBED
MOST COMMON SHOOTING ERROR

Pulls
shots
down
here.

It takes a while to learn proper, straight-to-the-rear trigger control. If you don't spend the time training, you will miss your target because untrained shooters tend to push a handgun's shots low and left. That's good to know if you have to run from someone shooting a pistol at you. Try not to run straight away, always run erratically and diagonally away from the shooter, toward the side of his shooting hand. That may cause his shots to land behind you.

SIGHTS PERFECTLY ALIGNED

White Dots for night

Regular notch 'n post

DRY FIRING

You need to educate your trigger finger. To train it, load your revolver with spent shells (dead primer, no powder or bullet). Cock the hammer and watch the sights carefully as you squeeze the trigger. Your trigger finger disturbed the sight alignment if the sights move just as the hammer falls. When you can squeeze the trigger without disturbing the sight alignment, even in the least, you're ready to begin firing live ammo.

Have a friend load three rounds in your revolver and hand you the weapon, (hammer down) so you don't know when those rounds will fire. Shoot six. Three times the hammer will fall on an empty chamber, which is your opportunity to train yourself to watch your sights carefully as the hammer falls. The other three rounds should surprise you when they go off. Since you're now watching the sights as the gun fires, you should be able to call where the bullet will land. If the real hole in the target is right where you think it should've been, then your trigger control has improved. But if you call the shot to land in one place and find a hole elsewhere, your trigger finger is shoving the barrel off just as the gun goes off. Work some more on dry firing. When you get control of your trigger, change your practice. Shoot at night, and shoot at body-sized targets, not bull's-eyes.

We push two kinds of training—-mental and physical—-with equal enthusiasm. Mechanical skills alone are not enough. Having the mental make-up to use those skills in combat is much more important. Learning a few moves with a baseball bat or how to shoot well is fine. Nevertheless, you **must** also train your mind to react promptly and forcibly to counter a violent threat.

66

"I certainly don't wish to spend whatever remaining time the Lord allows me on earth in the company of jailed convicts. But if the choice is being buried or being jailed, I'll accept jailed."

Craig Huber

Chapter 6

HOW TO DEFEND YOURSELF IN AND AROUND WHERE YOU LIVE

As you learned in training, preparation is your greatest friend. When trouble comes, you won't be able to think your way through a battle. The fight-or-flight syndrome takes over, and the brain (at least) simply leaves. So, what you do in the midst of battle has to be done by rote. You can't think about it—-you won't be able to anyway.

Without preparation, most violent confrontations in your home will cause you to panic, whereupon you lose. We think so many people panic because invasion of their home violates their psychological safe space. It's the same in the privacy of a vehicle. Almost everyone considers his or her car to be a private place. Intrusion into that space overloads sensitivity and therefore can cause panic. **Panic**, remember, is your greatest enemy in any defense situation.

PUTTING YOUR DEFENSE PLAN INTO EFFECT

After committing to your plan of defense, create safety in your home. Consider all the offensive possibilities you may need to defend, then plot to handle them. Timing counts. When a "defensive" situation arises it's almost always too late to think about how to deal with it. It's going to rain crime pretty soon; get your umbrella ready. First, do those things which don't require outside help or new equipment purchases. Don't wait for all the parts to come together. You may not have time. Do what you can immediately.

How about your defense plan? Does the whole family know about it? Do children know about the changes in your home and life style to accommodate your plan? Are your doors and windows secure? Does your defense plan include firearms? Is your weapon with you at home and loaded with the correct ammunition? Can you get to it right away in an emergency? Choose a sanctuary or safe room. Get it ready. Make a decision about your last line of defense. Your safe room entrance should provide a shooting line to all other sleeping areas.

To be prepared at all times, provide yourself with early warnings. Listen carefully to the sounds your house already makes. Squeaky doors or loose floorboards can be blessings and should be left to squeak if they provide information. Add some sound effects of your own to your home's surroundings. Small dogs generally sleep in your bedroom; they growl slightly when they hear something human ears can't detect. The result: you're awake and ready long before someone breaks into your home, but the perpetrator never heard the rumbling warning your dog gave you. Gravel beds just outside your downstairs windows are a good idea, too. Nobody can step there without making a crunch. You get the same effect in certain seasons of the year by raking leaves so they crunch if stepped on.

Note this: Where I might give up my life for my family or a close friend, I won't do that to protect things. I will let my possessions go as long as I am positive that by doing so I'm reducing the risk of injury or death. Of course, you may not be reducing risk by letting someone rob you. It's a judgment call.

TACTICAL HOUSE LIGHTING
Don't turn every light in the house on when you're going to be away, then turn out all the lights in the house when you're ready for bed. Most professional criminals pattern their victims. If you only leave outside lights on at night when you're away the crooks will have a perfect signal to let them know when the house is vacant. Vary the pattern of your activities as much as possible. Several companies make timer switches which vary the patterns for you.

EMERGENCY: HOUSE BURGLARY
You get a call; there's a severe emergency. You jump in the car, race to the hospital, and no emergency. When you get home, everything's gone. You get another call late at night stating your place of business has been broken into or is on fire. . .

Don't leave your home and family unguarded. If your loved one is already in the hospital, getting there five minutes later is going to make very little difference. Always check emergency calls. With a call-verifier gadget on your phone which you can now purchase from many telephone supply outlets, note the number from which the call originates. Otherwise, ask for the name and phone number of the caller and find out who (doctor, police officer, etc.) and where, they are. Call the number right back to verify and check the phone number against the supposed location.

WHEN SOMEONE COMES TO YOUR DOOR
Always identify law enforcement personnel by ID card as well as badge. Familiarize yourself with the ID cards of police, sheriffs, and federal law enforcement agencies. The above goes double for anyone who comes to your house not in uniform. Check them out before admitting them.

Post your front door: No solicitors. Never let any stranger into your home. Be it Bibles or bilge pumps, accept no salesmen without an appointment. Likewise, never admit strangers with emergencies, even with an apparent injury. It's like picking up hitch hikers. Your life and the lives of your family may depend on this. You can do them a favor; take a number and make a phone call for them.   Don't let them in or leave your door unlocked when you go to make a call. They may follow you into the house.

ON THE PHONE
Don't accept cold sales calls.   Even if they're selling something you really want, don't go for it. Any phone solicitor's boiler room employs some people who probably couldn't get a job anywhere else. Some companies will ship COD after the phone call whether or not you bought anything. Others will sell several items, charge the correct COD amount, and be long gone after you discover something you paid for wasn't packed in the box.

Of course, be very careful about giving personal information over the phone. Questions about income, finances or personal wealth get no answer. All inquiries from private investigators should get a hang up. Most investigators work for attorneys. At worst, they will sue you. At best, they'll subpoena you.

In addition to that, here's what **not** to do.   Make a recording for your phone answering machine that goes,

a.　　　"Hi, we're out of town for the next two weeks."
b.　　　"You have reached the Mulberries at 6224 Rip-off St."
c.　　　"You have reached 624-4567 at 2437 Haven Rd."
d.　　　"I sleep during the day, so I'll answer your call later."
e.　　　"We're probably out fishing."
f.　　　"If it's you, Sally, we left a key under the mat."

To the wrong person, here's how those messages translate: **a.** You have two weeks before anybody will know you broke in. **b.** Drive to this house and call from your car phone. If no one answers again break in. **c.** Phone number with house address. You can clear it for break-in later. **d.** Rapists delight. **e.** Check to see if the boat is gone too; then break in. **f.** My elevator doesn't go all the way up to the top.

DEALING WITH NUISANCE,
OBSCENE, OR THREATENING PHONE CALLS

HANG UP! Don't talk to the callers, don't threaten them or ask anything. Just hang up and call the operator, then police.   Don't wait for the second or third call. Act immediately after the first one.

Buy a call identifier. These little goodies tell you the phone number of anyone calling you. If you're having trouble with nuisance or obscene calls, and you don't have one, pretend.   "I have the number you're calling from on my call verifier. Stay there while I call the police." That should take care of the problem.

It's best not to list your number in the directory.   If you do, however, don't use your full name. As we all know, most single women who list in the directory use a first initial only.   It was a way to avoid obscene calls until perverts figured it out and started dialing first initial names.   Single men! You can do a big favor for hundreds of harassed women. If you list your phone, don't use your full first name—only your first initial.   That way, all the hot breath callers won't be able to pick women out of the phone book by first initial only. I thank you, my sister thanks you, and your next date will think you're kind and considerate.

LIKE HOWARD HUGHES---MAINTAIN PRIVACY

Many divorced spouses wish not to be discovered or disturbed by an ex-spouse. One of the highest levels of phone security you can achieve is to have your phone issued to a John Doe, be unlisted, and the number not widely known. Lesser levels achieve lesser security.

A client came to Don and said, "My husband owes thousands in child support and I can't locate him, but I know he's living in Washington State. I have his parent's phone number in New York, but they won't tell me where he is." So he called the parent's phone company and said, "This is Mr. Jones from 6224 Parchment, and my number at home is 234-5981. I'm on vacation at 640 Loma Circle. Could you send my next two phone bills to this address so I can pay my bill on time?" A week later, the first bill showed several calls to a number in area code 206 (Washington State). Bingo.

DEFENDING YOURSELF AT HOME

Think like a criminal while preparing your defense. React like a soldier while carrying it out. The greatest enemy in any stress situation is panic. The greatest cures for panic are preparation and training.

To develop an effective plan, first assess the various threats you're likely to face, both at home and on the street. How can you do this? The military calls the gathering of information about the situation, terrain around us, the enemy, his strengths, and his methods of operation intelligence. Without that information, you may make some bad decisions.

WHAT DO YOU NEED TO KNOW?

Is your neighborhood attractive to house burglars? Why? Can the situation be changed or improved? Is there a convicted sex offender living in the immediate area? Is the incidence of assault, robbery, or rape on the increase or decrease? These are questions you need answers to before you can begin your defense planning.

Other questions are important, too. Is your neighborhood near a major civil disturbance site? Are you close to a state fair ground or carnival site? Is a convention center or high rent business district close by? Is your neighborhood located near a rock concert site? All of these factors can elevate the threat level to an area because of the transients they attract.

Where can you find out all that you need to know about any city? Of course, check the yellow pages. Adult movies and pawnshops are normally located in areas you should avoid at night. That's where all the scum slinks. Check that area out on your map. In the library, check the local paper's "police blotter" or "crime corner" column. If the paper

71

is on microfiche, it's easy to read how things have gone for the last few months. No matter where you are, foreign countries or small towns, the best, low-down gossip is always obtainable at the local beauty parlor. Book an appointment, get a shampoo and cut, and spend some time listening to your hair stylist. She knows enough about the neighborhood to earn a living as a local gossip columnist.

Individual police officers may be a valuable source of information. They can tell you about the level and kinds of crime in a neighborhood. The police reports, which you have a right to see, will give you good insight on the local violent crime situation.

Your future neighbors can be a great source of local intelligence. Visit them and ask a few questions about what goes on in the area. A quick trip around the neighborhood will tell you a lot, too. Look and listen. Are the homes generally in a good state of repair. Is the greenery trimmed, trash picked up? A neighborhood allowed to deteriorate is often an indication of trouble. Are there junked cars in the yards? Are adult males loitering during working hours? Do you hear sounds of domestic unrest? How do older children react to you? Are they respectful, or surly? Tatoos of similar kinds, kids hanging around together doing nothing, and cars doctored up to ride low are signs of rebellion and gang membership which indicate you should live elsewhere. Are young children open and friendly—-or fearful and remote? Do many of the homes have alarm systems? Are the police friendly, or are they cautious and distant?

One final death sign: Graffiti. If you see any of it anywhere, you know gangs are within walking distance. This spray painting on walls is the same thing your dog does on bushes. The only thing worse than graffiti is graffiti crossed out or overwritten. You'll see one sign crossed out with a "no" next to it, and a rival gang sign over that with the word "si" next to it. That spells "disrespectful challenge," and it means the locals will soon make stronger statements punctuated by periods—of gunfire. Your home may not be air conditioned, but we can guarantee it'll soon be ventilated.

I took a wrecked late model Volkswagen to Tijuana for repairs. In the same shop, I discovered a brand new Toyota pickup with over 280 bullet holes in it. Nobody killed. It was merely a warning over a gang dating dispute.

CHOOSING A PLACE TO LIVE---LOCATION, LOCATION

With security in mind, don't choose a home simply for a view, the house, the acreage or the school zone. What makes a neighborhood good or bad has only to do with the people who live there and the frequent passers-by. Before you buy, spend a lot of time in the neighborhood. Walk around and talk to people. As in Vietnam during the war, many neighborhoods change radically after dark—-but most homes are shown by agents during the day only. Would you be safe taking a walk near this home after dark? Many people live under the constant fear of crime in American neighborhoods.

Professional thieves don't just drive into a neighborhood at random and start robbing houses. They may "case" an area for days before making a move. It makes sense to use this same technique and patience to choose your home. Learn what a burglar looks for. Then buy the opposite.

Think about this. The enemy is out there, and they're looking for plunder. You want your house to be a less attractive target than the houses of your neighbors. If the enemy is going to target a house, an individual, or victim, he will most often choose the target easiest to hit. Anything you can do to make the criminal think this house or person is more difficult will be a step in the right direction.

You can't eliminate risk; you merely reduce it. Load the odds in your favor. Even the United States Secret Service, the acknowledged world leader in personal security, doesn't presume to guarantee the safety of the President. Their goal is to reduce the risk to the greatest degree possible. This has to be your goal also.

Ask a local agent what auto insurance will cost if you buy in a certain area. In some suburbs, auto insurance premiums are out of sight unless a theft exclusion is written in the policy. Insurance rates in Santa Barbara (70 miles North) cost about half of the L.A. rates. Insurance companies can also tell you about house burglaries. Compare premiums for home content insurance. Higher premiums for comparable coverage indicate a higher level of risk.

Is your house interior visible from the street? Privacy sheer curtains allow you to see out, but keep you invisible as long as there is more light outside. Are all the doors and ground floor windows clear of shielding shrubs or fencing? Trim your trees to provide three feet of clearance from the lowest branch to the ground. You don't want to provide a shield for burglars to hide behind while they work to get past your doors and windows. Neither do you want to provide an ambush site for a personal attack.

Organize your neighborhood. Make the whole neighborhood less attractive to criminals so they go elsewhere. Neighborhood Watch programs really are taking a bite out of crime.

ELECTRONIC DATA TAKEN BY
CASUAL CITIZEN ADMISSABLE IN PROSECUTION

Wolf ears and long distance zoom cameras used by casual citizens can now easily record drug deals by crack dealers, prostitution solicitations, and various assaults as they did in the Rodney King case.

In the military intelligence business, anything broadcast over the airwaves is free and usable information. Should something out of a criminals mouth be private when we think we're waging a war on crime? We need new laws to make such information automatically in public domain. Therefore, it will be admissible as evidence in criminal trials. Second, we need to pay a reward for the information. It will turn thousands of citizens into private eyes, convict huge numbers of crack and other drug dealers, and be far cheaper than paying police salaries.

Does your house stand out from neighbors' houses? Does it look richer or easier to break into? Are there areas from which your home can be watched without the watcher being seen and attracting attention? Can your house be approached from more than one direction by someone in a vehicle? Can a vehicle be parked near your home and not be visible to your neighbors or from a passing patrol?

Answer this: How would you get into your house if you locked yourself out? Can you make your home much less accessible to an intruder and still allow for emergency entry by yourself? What can you do for yourself and for what will you need outside help? Can you count on yourself to deal with most confrontations or should you consider ways to summon help? Let security take priority over convenience or comfort. The next time you consider buying a new toy for your house, think first whether or not you can protect it.

Develop your security plan around your own abilities. Do you have previous firearms experience? Are there religious convictions which might stop you from acting? Be realistic as you assess your strengths and weaknesses. Are you strong enough, equipped to fight, and well enough trained? Can you run? Could you get yourself in condition? Can you correct the problems you find in and around your home? Will the cost be prohibitive? If so, is a move possible?

Start your home defense planning with pen and paper. Start a quarter mile from your home and work your way back home in rough circles. Walk around; make notes. You miss too much if you drive.

SETTING GOALS

As in many things, the simplest plan is often best. Set defense goals and be specific. Think, "I want to reduce the risk of having my home burglarized, having my children molested, having a violent confrontation in or near my home, or having my car stolen, broken into, or vandalized. I want to increase my chances of coming out the winner in any confrontation I can't avoid."

A useful set of goals might read like this:
To develop a defense plan for both my family and our home.
To reduce the risks of becoming a victim of violence.
To reduce the risks of being a victim of thieves or burglars.
To make my home less attractive to criminals.
To increase my chances of winning any violent confrontation I can't avoid.

Prepare to do **whatever is necessary** to accomplish your goals. Be advised: You may have to kill. Be sure you're prepared to do that or your defense plan could become useless. Worse, it could turn a bad situation into a lethal situation with an outcome exactly opposite of your plan. If you pick up a weapon and think you can get by with bluffing, think again. The criminal has lived and survived on the streets for years. In a New York minute, they can discern the difference between your fear and your very real threat of force.

**PRACTICE YOUR PLAN.   THEN AVOID ALL THE TROUBLE
YOU POSSIBLY CAN.**

Plan to avoid a violent personal confrontation whenever possible, but prepare to deal with any confrontation you can't avoid, and win it——decisively!

75

TO PREVENT CRIME RE-OCCURRENCE
IMPLANTS FOR CONVICTS AS A CONDITION OF PAROLE

Modern medicine and the electronic age make it now possible to prevent a large percentage of crimes. To secure release from prison, criminals promise society to make no further assault. If we make a treaty with another country, we inspect and thereby prove their good faith performance. Why not do the same with criminals? How can a criminal make himself available for inspection so society can guarantee no more assaults will occur? As a condition of release and as good faith in performing their "never again" covenant, a prisoner should accept an implant. Implants go just under the skin in a harmless capsule, and emit a code, chemical, or pain when activated electronically. For example:

1. Child abusers wear an implant activated by electronic signals sent from transmitters of limited range located on school grounds.

2. Rapists wear a pain-producing implant which can be activated by a victim in fear. When the victim flees, the pain subsides because of increased distance from the victim's code transmitter.

3. Bank robbers. Implant prevents entry into banks.

4. Drug addicts. Implant produces pain upon contact with drugs in blood.

5. Gun violators. Implant produces pain around gun blast.

6. Drunk Drivers. Implant produces severe pain when activated by alcohol in bloodstream, plus car motion.

Arguments: Citizens have rights to life, liberty and pursuit of happiness. Those rights in jeopardy outweigh rights of criminals, who by their voluntary acts have chosen to diminish or take away other citizens' rights. Also, the parolee accepts the implant as a condition of freedom. Implants don't eliminate freedom; they restrict freedom in those areas where the criminal has already demonstrated his penchant for abuse.

Chapter 7

HOW TO DEFEND VEHICLES
AGAINST THEFT AND CARJACKING.

THE FASTEST GROWING CRIME—CARJACKING

More and more crime occurs to people while in and around vehicles. Rental car agencies now charge as much as $17 per day for insurance, a large part of which is for theft.

"But I always lock my rental car at night and park it in a well lit spot," I argued.

"Yes, but this insurance is for armed vehicle robbery," was the reply.

Carjacking is a crime in which the enemy gets your car, your purse, and all the property you keep in your car. *USA TODAY* wrote in October, 1992 that carjacking has become a rite of passage for gang members. The germs steal your car, then drive it around for a few days to show off. Of course, some do it for money. In a chop shop, parts off your car are worth four times the value of the vehicle.

LOSING YOUR CAR WHILE DRIVING IT

Here's one way: You stop at a traffic light. Two germs team up. One steps off the curb in front of your car just as the light turns yellow. The other comes up from behind. With his back turned to traffic behind you, he taps on your window with a pistol and orders you out of the car. You get out quickly and run for your life. He jumps in and drives off. You think you should call for police to report your car stolen, but you really need to send the police to your home. Why? Attached to your car keys are your home keys, and your auto registration in the glove compartment carries your home address. He may go there next. Quick; call home! Warn your family!

Take precautions against carjacking. For starters, detach your car keys from your house keys. Use a post office box mailing address on your auto registration. Memorize your license number.

Of course, improve your rear vision. Don't drive a car without a rear view mirror on the passenger side. It's a good idea to install a multi-window rear view mirror so you can see all your blind spots. Mine's a WINK, from Pep Boys. If someone steps off the curb in front of you, drive ahead slowly. The LAPD advises, "You're not driving your vehicle over someone if they have a chance to get out of the way." Once you see a move toward a weapon, step on the gas and go. If you're parked right behind someone's bumper, you'll have trouble getting away. To prevent carjacking at a stoplight, leave some maneuvering space between you and the car ahead, say, half a car length. Practice that. You need to develop the habit.

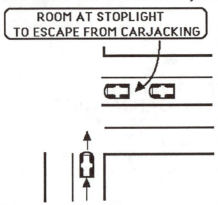

ROOM AT STOPLIGHT
TO ESCAPE FROM CARJACKING

On occasion, someone steals a police car and rapes women who pull over in a dark area after the perp flashes red lights. Any doubts? Don't stop in a dark area; drive slowly ahead to a well lit, crowded area.

You're most vulnerable to attack just as you get into, or out of, your car. That's when the germs like to hold you up at gun point, which can happen in a variety of circumstances. Perhaps they follow you out of a shopping mall. As you get to the car, they attack. Rest stops and gas stations are also ambush places where the germs attack. Chances of being robbed go up in places such as poorly lit parking lots after hours and underground parking garages where you have to venture alone.

Perps know your back is turned while you're opening your door. You can fix that. 1. Tint your side windows and keep them clean so you can use them as a mirror. 2. Check your perimeter before you approach your car. 3. Don't look at your door lock. Stand back at arms length and scan the reflections in your car door windows. Look for movement. Soften your focus; don't stare at one spot on your window, but try and see the <u>whole</u> window all at once. Thus, you'll be able to see anything on both sides of your reflected body.

Some of the most heinous crimes occur when someone follows the victim home. If they get you in the driveway, they get you, your house keys, five minutes of frantic shopping in your house, and your car. That's quite a rite of passage. To prevent this from happening, we developed the **rule of four turns**. From now on as you drive home, identify the car behind you. During the day you can observe the make, model, and occupants. During the night, you have to rely on street lights or close examination of the headlight-parking light

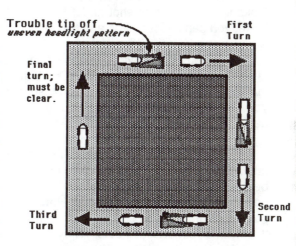

CARJACKING

How to give followers the slip with the rule of four turns.

Trouble tip off — *uneven headlight pattern*

First Turn

Final turn; must be clear.

Third Turn

Second Turn

configuration on the car behind you. Check to see if maybe one is out of adjustment with the other. How wide set are the lights in the car? Silhouette the occupants behind back lighting and memorize the pattern; take notice of hats, hair, head heights, etc.

Now—<u>make four right turns.</u> If the same car is behind you when you come back out on your original route, you have a problem. Drive to a police station, a highway patrol office, or the busiest gas station you know. But, **don't** drive home. Incidentally, besides checking all the time to see who is following you, make a habit of taking a quick look in the back seat before you climb into the car so you don't get in with a stowaway germ.

The germs also have a clever way of getting you out of your car while you're driving in traffic. They bump into you from behind. Knowing it's not your fault and being the good citizen you are, you step out right away to exchange insurance papers. According to the LAPD, the advice on what to do in that situation has been changed. Now you drive slowly and in orderly fashion to a crowded gas station. Then step out. Otherwise, you'll step out into a crime as the driver who bumped into you deliberately jumps into your vehicle and drives away. One more caution: Don't let anybody come up to clean your windshield. If someone approaches with a spray bottle and towel, turn your windshield wipers on and warn him away.

When you're out of the car with a firearm on your person, and it looks like you may be shot at, hit the deck and roll under a car. Once there, you can shoot at legs and feet without taking serious return fire.

If you don't have a weapon and you're not prepared to shoot, Listen to the words of the LAPD: "Don't give up your privacy." Don't get into any car at gun point; don't allow someone to get into the car with you. If a perp tries to force you into a car, just faint; go limp and become deadweight.

It's hard to know where the next ambush will be or the form it will take. During one ten-day period in Oakland, California, 15 victims were beaten, shot at and robbed at the corner of 26th Street and Treat, a government project housing area. How? The oil can caper. The germs poured oil on the road so cars spun out; then they attacked and beat on the victims with baseball bats. They shot several others. Also new and becoming popular is this: The germ goes into a restaurant or store and tells management, "Arizona License # DPJ-378, a tan, 92 Mercedes left the headlights on." Remedy: Think, "did I really leave my lights on?" Don't get up; it's an ambush. The germs are out in the parking lot--- waiting for you. At gun point, they take your keys, then drive off in your Mercedes. Stores, quit broadcasting unless you confirm.

Just as some kinds of vehicles attract more criminals than others, so do some drivers. High-ticket foreign sports cars offer the most tempting targets. If you buy one of these, ask the dealer if it also comes with a high-ticket pistol. Female drivers attract more crime than males do. They're thought of as weaker and easier victims. Also, the possibility of rape appeals to criminals. Also, carjackers prefer single occupants. unless the other is a child, in which case, they often threaten the child's life if you don't comply with their demands. Don't take these threats lightly. If they threaten you and don't follow through, they lose peer acceptance.

Huber's primary vehicle is a pickup truck. He had an auxiliary gas tank installed to extend his cruising range to over 500 miles. Make a point of keeping the spare tank full. If you go the pickup route, consider a lift kit and big tires. Southland Corp. cut robberies in its 7-11 stores by raising the cash registers so robbers couldn't see the loot. In a perpetrator's mind, bigger trucks with tinted windows make vehicle robbery a lot riskier.

PURCHASING CONSIDERATIONS

The average person probably won't make defense from crime a number one priority when choosing a vehicle. Regardless of the kind of car you buy, it will be safer with certain options: Think security. Consider power windows and power door locks. Power steering and anti-lock brakes give you an advantage when maneuvering defensively.

Get a sturdy, heavy-duty vehicle with plenty of carrying capacity and a large fuel tank. You may have to evacuate your home during a civil disorder or natural disaster. Can you transport your whole family and the items you'll need for survival and comfort?

Along with all of the above, there are lots of things you can do to make your car safer and more theft proof. First, consider car burglary. Somebody wants your stereo, CB, tires, wheels, etc. Defense: Leave nothing visible. Remember, most theft occurs as opportunity presents itself. Never think your car is safe. Keep your car's interior sterile of things to steal, even while underway. Mount your CB under the seat or in a compartment overhead.

How about car theft itself? A locking device (like the Club) across your steering wheel helps, but you have to place it so the key inserts from the dash board side. Don't put the lock on your steering wheel with the lock pointing at the driver's seat. Otherwise, a car thief who just drilled the lock on your car door can use the same drill on the club.

A fuel shutoff prevents the car thief from driving far away. Kill switches and alarms are also good. We've examined both the *Clifford and Viper Alarm* systems and found them to be excellent. Most will sound off only after your vehicle is disturbed by severe motion.

Keep your vehicle in first-class running condition. If your car breaks down, you may get robbed. At a minimum, make sure your tires are in good shape, all the belts are sound and the fluid levels are up to par. Have your vehicle checked regularly and perform the recommended oil changes, lubrication, and regular tune ups. An oil treatment such as *Slick 50* will cut wear on your engine and allow you to drive it for a short time with any junk lubrication in it. We think the American Automobile Association is a great bargain. You can call for help if your car breaks down.

AVOID SOLITARY CONFINEMENT

Without any communication to the outside world, you're an isolated prisoner when you drive. At least carry a sign for your window which says, "CALL POLICE." Better yet, install a CB radio and learn to use it. Channel nine (REACT) is often manned by base station operators who offer help and directions. Truckers routinely hang out on channel 17 & 19. You can learn to use a CB radio easily, and thereafter, help is only a push button away. Be careful though; anything you send over the airwaves could reach the wrong ears. If you give your location over the radio, use direction, highway number, and closest mile marker (police procedure). One good place to install your CB is under your seat if you have room. Thieves normally don't steal what they can't see. Another is in the packaged ceiling kits you can get from automotive and RV mail order houses such as **J.C. Whitney**, who will send you a catalog if you call **312-431-6102**. If you're poor, drive a jalopy, and can't afford a radio or telephone, look around at garage sales for a microphone cord and let it hang loosely out of your dash. Most thieves will think your car is an undercover DEA buggy.

Iinstall a cellular phone in your vehicle so you can call if someone starts hassling you on the road. Also, you can summon help without leaving your vehicle and putting yourself at greater risk in the event of mechanical failure. Use a police and emergency scanning unit in your car. Information you get over that radio let's you avoid bank robberies in progress, bad traffic accidents, and severe fires; plus, you get the latest news on new crime.

HIDING

Tint your car's windows. Your local dealer knows how dark you can go. I prefer a bit darker. What you want is a window which hides you and your loved ones from easy observation by criminals. A lot of random violence never occurs because the perpetrator is unsure of his victim's capability for retaliation. Along with that line of reasoning, don't drive alone; get a mannequin or large doll for the passenger seat.

Whether walking or driving, getting lost can create a situation in which you become a victim. Install a GuideTech compass in your car to help you choose alternate routes. Also, in *Great Livin' in Grubby Times,* we spent pages teaching you how to modify your car for survival. One good idea: Install kevlar inside your door panels to make them bullet proof.

DRIVING STRATEGY

Women, especially, should drive with a LIFO companion. LIFO means Last In, First Out, and that's how your passenger boards the vehicle. Men, quit driving. Let your wives drive; you ride shotgun. You can easily equip your car with a variety of pastime devices, including TV, stereo, AM radio, Bible, magazines or games to help pass the time if you have to wait. If you possibly can, go everywhere in pairs.

PREVENTING CARJACKING

DRIVE AROUND GAS STATION IN A CIRCLE TO CHECK FOR BUMS AND GANGS BEHIND

SIDEWALK

STREET

PUMPS

Park
and
fill
here

GAS
STATION
BUILDING

Travel direction

Carjacking from gas stations is also popular. I guess it beats robbing the station for $200. If you drive into a station at night, drive around behind it before you stop at the pumps. You drive into a parking lot or a gas station the same way a military patrol would come into an operational area. This is routine. Scouts set up a perimeter. In this case, the man is the scout, and the perimeter is the area around the car. The man gets out of the car while the engine is still running and checks things out. If he comes under attack, he can either dive back into the car or return fire as the driver gets away. But the driver doesn't travel very far. She has options. She can call for help, raise hell with the car horn and lights, turn on a siren, play bumper cars with perpetrators on foot, or get far enough away and open fire with a long range weapon. As Oprah frequently says nowadays, "It's getting rough out there, folks."

Don't pull over and stop just because someone signals to you on a highway. One of the new ruses to maneuver you into a position where you can be attacked goes like this: They roll down their window on the highway, or signal to you frantically to pull over because your tire is flat, or whatever. When you do, they pull up behind you as if to help, but they help themselves---to your car and person.

Another clever trick: The germs get a girlfriend with a baby to pull over to the side of the road and put the hood up. When you get out of your car to help, the perps come out of the bushes. Being a Good Samaritan is now a risky business.

SURVIVAL KIT FOR VEHICLES
Purchase a container for extra things you need in your car. A plastic, seal-tight box is inexpensive. Airtight food containers are my favorite because they are just the right size and waterproof. Fill the box with survival goodies. A cheap pair of binoculars in your car enables you to read and record license numbers plus analyze a situation from a safe distance away.

Once you have a container or two, use bags to separate the things you need to store. Old shaving kit bags hold tools. Nylon zipper bags (fanny packs) hold material you might take with you on a hike. Below is a partial list of some things you might want with you.
Personal survival.
Drinking water. One gallon per passenger. Think also about your radiator.

Food. Make sure what you take won't spoil. Dried fruits, nuts, and seeds in a sealable container will work. Buy a few pounds of a trail mix mixture and replace it once in a while.

Clothes. Old boots are great. You can always get a few extra miles out of them, and you won't have to break them in during your emergency. You normally wear shoes in your car but, if your car breaks down, you may find yourself walking a long distance over rough terrain, so you'll need boots. In cold weather, it's absolutely essential to carry an MPI™ space blanket. They conserve 80% of your body heat and cost less than $15—good insurance. These space blankets will also save your bacon from frying in desert heat. You make a tarp out of them with the silver side up and crawl into the shade underneath. Add a stainless steel, lockback folding **Mamba Blackjack** knife. The factory keeps them razor sharp for you. Also, maybe add a Gerber Multi-plier.

Buy a First Aid kit and put it in a waterproof bag. Make sure your kit includes an air splint. They don't cost a lot, but most severe wrecks in vehicles require these. Training for first aid is best done by taking a red cross class. If you do it all at home, you can use a video tape, *Medicine for the Outdoors,* by Paul Auerbach, M.D.

Buy a roll of quarters for emergencies and install them on the outside of your air filter in the air cleaner under your hood. You can keep spare keys there also unless your hood latch is inside the car. In that event, you have to hide a key outside the car, but only the one which opens the doors. Lose your keys? The Hide-a-key gets you into the car. The hood latch gets you the ignition key so you can drive home.

<u>Vehicle survival.</u>

Fluids. Your car needs transmission fluid, (for emergencies, will work in engine also) motor oil, and coolant (water). Aluma-seal comes in a small package a little larger than a roll of quarters. If you get a bullet hole in your radiator, you can pour the seal in when the water is hot and the seal will plug the leaks.

Spare parts. Belts, hoses, worm drive hose clamps, bulbs, seal beams, old rotor, and a couple old spark plugs. Just save the old ones when you install new. Buying new ones and leaving them in your trunk can cause this problem: You suffer an emergency or enemy attack. To avoid the problem, you strain your vehicle to the max at high speed or on rough ground. A radiator hose or water pump belt gives out. You hurry to install the new one, but it's the wrong size! Put new ones on the car; old ones in the trunk.

Tools. Again, old ones. Just make sure to use them before you toss them in the trunk. Don't buy new junkers. Garage sale it and put together a set of good old (perhaps Craftsman?) tools you can rely on. Try 4 screw drivers, (two Phillips), three pliers (needle, water pump, and regular) 3/8th's drive socket set, open end/box end wrenches, 2 crescent wrenches, and some hammers. You may need to pound a fender away from a tire so you can drive away.

A pre-packed roadside trouble kit which contains flares, jumper cables and a flashlight. Tow rope. A used come-along (about $10).

Test your car's jack to make sure it works and you're familiar with its use.

Install a locking gas cap. They not only keep thieves from stealing your gas, but nobody can put foreign material into your tank, thus causing your engine to die while they follow you from a shopping mail.

Don't go anywhere without fix-a-flat. It not only fixes slow leaks by re-sealing the tire-to-rim bead, but it saves time you may have to spend on the road changing a flat.

Look into a defensive driving school. Bob Bondurant (Bondoo-rhant) has an excellent school located in Phoenix. Other schools scattered around the country teach advanced driving technique. These schools can be tough on vehicles, so it's a good idea to rent one similar to your own for school. Of course, get full insurance.

Former Hollywood Stuntwomens' Association President Sunny Woods attended that school and offered this advice: *"Pump up the tires with a can of easy flat repair you get from most auto parts stores. Use four cans. Remove the hub caps and tape them together in the trunk of your car. You'll be sliding sideways and you don't want to lose a hub cap or have a tire collapse because you don't have enough bead-to-rim tire pressure."*

Do not leave your auto registration in your glove compartment or over your visor. That used to be the accepted practice; no more. In former times, auto registration was required. Today's computers prove you own the car. If you carry yours in the vehicle, use a plastic baggie, and hide it. For example, you may want to bury it under the rubber mats in the trunk, or tape it up under the dash in a tough place to find. Why? Same reason you hide your garage door opener. Thieves in shopping malls search for garage door openers on the visor of your car. One flick of the wrist, and they smash your car

86

window with a chip. Then they either take the car, or merely remove the opener with your registration, which may have your true street address on it. Later on, you'll wonder how someone drove right into your garage, burglarized your house, and left so quickly.

Personalized license plates are a bad idea, especially for women. They're too easy to remember and they might give some psycho a twitch. Lot's of rapes occur because they give the rapist a feeling of conquest. Important women with personalized plates may appear to be a bigger conquest. You don't want to attract attention to yourself or your car. For the same reason, don't have any "BABY ON BOARD" signs in the windows, (invites kidnappers). Any confrontational bumper stickers or signs might make a redneck mad.

Express yourself at the polls, not on the public highway. Remember how religion and politics are to be avoided in polite conversation? To avoid controversy, keep the rear bumper or back window of your family van clean. You never know what is going to set off some already-troubled half-wit. Keep in mind that a large percentage of the lower class jerks you see on the road use physical violence to win conflicts with wives at home. Why should it be any different with you?

Go out of your way not to offend anyone on the road. But if you do make a mistake, your chances of becoming involved in a violent confrontation remain less when you haven't posted additional insults on your bumper.

WHEN GUNS ARE OUTLAWED ...

Why don't the lawmakers believe the bumper stickers? Some state legislatures vote to make life sweet for criminals. California, for example, acknowledges 27,000 felons who own illegal weapons. The other 50,000 felonious weapons owners belong to gangs, and they don't report gun ownership.

... ONLY OUTLAWS WILL HAVE GUNS.

FIREARMS IN THE VEHICLE

Keep at least one defensive firearm in your vehicle at all times. Do everything you can to avoid a violent confrontation but be prepared to defend yourself. Whatever defense weapons you choose to bring with you, take a supply of ammo. Don't just throw some shells in the car. Take Sunday go-to-meetin' super-stoppers. Mix 'n match so you load the weapon for war rather than birds or target shooting.

Don't expect to get special treatment as a good citizen if you get caught with a weapon in the car. Many California prosecutors are into numbers the same way Lyndon Johnson was into body count. Whether they catch a gang member or a citizen violating gun laws doesn't matter; a conviction is a conviction. A gang member goes to prison to be with his friends—but your conviction sends you into a hostile atmosphere. Therefore, gang members don't care about gun laws, but good citizens have real reason to obey. To a cop, an arrest is an arrest. For these reasons, **never** give permission to anyone to search your vehicle for any reason. The cop will be an expert at making you feel guilty. Just don't give in. No matter if you car is sterile---don't give permission to search! Later, they may search anyway and find a machine gun. (How did that get there?) But an attorney can have that evidence returned to you later as inadmissable because you didn't waive your rights.

The question you think you have to answer is: Should you carry a weapon in the car with you? But that's the wrong question. The correct question is: If you do carry a weapon in your car, will you use it? To do that, you'll have to overcome your fear of jail, your good humanistic inhibitions, and a lack of proficiency with the firearm. Don't avoid thinking your way through the issue. Here's why: If you don't want to use a weapon, don't carry it in the car. Without practice and firm mental resolve, a weapon is a liability. If someone points his weapon at you and you decide to draw yours, God help you. It's best to do what the perp demands. Do you think you're going to be shot anyway? Never say die. You'll need lots of practice and a great holster from Eagle, but you may beat a perp who doesn't suspect you're armed.

In a personal interview with the LAPD, the Downtown Division Crime Prevention officer told us this: After the riot in South Central, people in L. A. were buying weapons in record numbers. But few practice enough to be familiar and quick with the weapons they buy. Moreover, people who buy the weapons "are too humanistic" to be able to kill another human easily. Therefore, there is a lag time by good people before they fire, but a hard-hearted, drugged-up enemy kills without hesitation. One more important reason for the critical lag time is this: Good citizens don't know the law but have an idea from what politicians send through the media that anyone who uses a gun is wrong. The enemy, on the other hand, has already had a good taste of how society punishes criminals and they're not afraid. If they feel afraid, they often take a drug to overcome the fear. Thus you can believe, in any gun battle with a criminal, you'll come out second best unless you practice and develop a hardened mind set.

How does the LA. Police Dept. define practice? "Shoot a thousand rounds a year." Better than a mere thousand rounds punching holes through paper, pistol shooting instructor Stuart Meredith says, "Practice has to put pressure on the student. The idea is to force the secretion of adrenaline by approximating real excitement." I agree. When you practice, try to prepare yourself for the heart-pounding fear you'll face in a real encounter.

All this book (any book) can do is provide information. We encourage you to practice and develop speed and resolve. If you have to shoot, avoid going to jail by doing what a criminal might do after it happens. Even if you make some mistakes and the other side lives to concoct a great lie in court under oath, think about this:

Better to be judged by twelve than carried by six.
(Pall bearers).

If you decide to carry a weapon, improve your driving habits. Don't do anything which might require an officer to search you or your vehicle. Of course, don't drink and drive. Never allow any passenger to open a container in your car. Keep documentation for the vehicle in proper order. Keep your home state concealed weapons carry permit current. When stopped by a police officer, it's a good idea to roll down your driver's side window and put both hands out into the light. Lay your wrists over the window ledge, which shows you have no evil intentions and puts the officer at ease. Never argue! They don't need the experience and the job doesn't pay any better because of flak they take from you. Always be polite and courteous when questioned. If you disagree with him or her, argue in court.

Now, after reading this, if you've decided to carry a weapon with you in your vehicle, let's think about what it should be. First, are you big and strong, or small and weak? The reason you need to answer is this: Many people buy bigger weapons for their car than they can handle comfortably on their person. Bigger caliber weapons can tempt you because they punch through cars and you don't have to carry the weight personally. But people put off practice when they own a big banger.

Lack of practice   increases your lag time in a confrontation. Bad idea.
Just buy what you know you can shoot without fear and practice---a lot.

Handgun or shotgun? For vehicle travel, you need to operate
your weapon with one hand so handguns are best. Reduced length
shotguns with folding stocks are OK, but only if you ride as passenger.

Driving alone. Wrap the pistol in a flimsy cloth to disguise it.
You can shoot right through any knit or sock. Once you've accessed the
weapon, it will look like a sock or some kind of knitting in your hand.
Hopefully, you won't have to shoot, and nobody will notice it. Another
way to carry is under the seat in a (cigar?) box. Put a piece of cord to
the box and attach the end of the cord to velcro near your feet. That
way, a short pull on the cord puts the weapon where you can grab it
easily, but it normally stays back, out of sight.

What about pistol caliber? We like the .357 magnum revolver
because its projectiles are capable of penetrating car bodies, which may
be necessary to stop attackers in a vehicle. We pass on automatics
because autos bounce hot shell casings off your windshield. Also, a
malfunction problem with an auto takes two hands to correct, which is
difficult during evasive driving.

Call **Lock and Load Distributors,** 703/289-6892 and
MasterCard 6 rounds for $15. The company will send you a package of
Annihiliators (they explode when they hit) or ™ CorBons (which
penetrate with super power). Perhaps the best is their Beehive bullet,
(104 gr. @ 1275 fps.; 9" into gel and 5" diameter wound cavity) which
turns inside out and spreads lead shot all over a target upon impact.
When you load a .38 like this, it becomes a much more effective
weapon. Mix 'n match loads so your handgun becomes more effective
for defense.

Most shotguns are LIFO loaders. LIFO means Last In, First Out.
The last round you load will be the first to fire. The first round in will be
last out. Also, the first round loaded in will be the last to fire.

Load accordingly. In a close range confrontation, you'll want
shot first, slugs later. In your house, you won't want to penetrate a wall
with a load of shot. Rifled slugs are heaviest and therefore penetrate
well. Double ought (00-Buck) buck loads are commonly used by prison

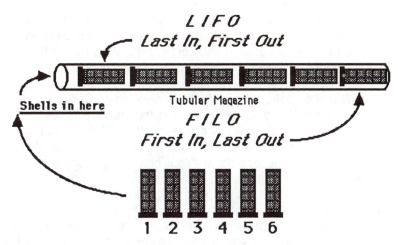

LIFO
Last In, First Out

Shells in here   Tubular Magazine

FILO
First In, Last Out

1 2 3 4 5 6

guards. They shoot nine .30 caliber balls, each lethal, and the spread of the shot is sure to score somewhere on a target. The best shotgun load for home defense is a high base shell with a load of two's or four's. For vehicles, however, you may need more distance and pentration. Go to double-ought Buck---9 rounds balls, each .30 caliber.

LAPD warns: "Turn up your perception knob." Listen to this from the bodyguard. Recently he was guarding a young girl from a royal family as she shopped in a Washington, D.C. mall. She handed him some packages to carry. He politely refused, and explained, "It's not that I wouldn't carry these, but I can't do my job if my hands are full."

When you come out of a shopping mall, your hands will probably be full, too. First, check the perimeter---the area around the store. Is anybody paying more attention to you than you deserve? If you sense trouble, go back into the mall and see if a security guard will watch you get into your car. If you go it alone, consider a shopping cart. They make folding ones now that you can carry into a store with you. That means only one hand is occupied with packages, and you can drop the handle easily to react to a situation. Do you suspect you're being followed while still on foot? If you have the time to get into your car and get away, do that. But if your stalker is close, opening your own car door is not a good idea. Act as if you can't find your car and make three consecutive right or left turns. If the same person is behind you, get ready for war. Walk towards others because there is safety in numbers. Duck behind a van or truck to get your weapon(s) ready. Failing that, start attracting attention. See if you can't work your way back into the mall where you can call for security.   Never act scared. Don't ignore the threat. If you can't slip back into the mall or move near a crowd, it's frontal assault time. Turn around and confront the stalker. Tell him you have a gun, shoot well, and are about to blow him away.

Don't make deals. Criminals lie convincingly. Don't ever think you can do what this person tells you and thus save yourself.   You can't be kind to them and expect kindness in return. If you're already in your car and you're told to move over, and let the perp into the driver's seat, **don't!** Step on the gas hard! Your chances of surviving being shot at while in a moving vehicle are good to excellent. Don't let anyone get in the car with you. But if it happens and he orders you to drive, just get nervous and crash into another car, preferably in the presence of a cop.. With this new set of circumstances, the perpetrator has some tough choices. He can shoot you in front of a crowd or get out and run.

PROBABILITY OF FUTURE CRIMES ASSIGNED FOR SENTENCING AND PAROLE.

Every criminal's category (armed robbery, burglary) and history will give a reasonable indication on the likelihood of his future offenses. Similar to insurance actuarial tables, that information can be graphed to give you a likely projection of what adverse affect his performance in society will have. Those tables must become a factor in sentencing, parole, and how much victim insurance a convict would be required to purchase. If bad driver's should pay higher insurance rates as assigned risks, how much more should a convict pay?

What if you're being followed in your car?   As we've written, don't drive home. Be patient. Look for a place with a lot of traffic, such as a supermarket parking lot. Perhaps drive through the isles of a gas station. Create interference if you can; maybe get a couple cars in between you.

The first step towards self defense in a vehicle is neither expensive nor difficult to learn. **Lock your car doors. Always**! If your windows are tinted well and your doors are locked, nobody can get into your car or see you. Your car is actually a fairly secure fortress if you make sure the doors are locked. An added benefit: Locking your doors will help prevent you from being thrown from the vehicle in the event of an accident. It also keeps children from accidentally opening the car door while under way.

Buckle your seat belt. It helps you stay in control if you have to do a bit of defensive driving. If someone does open your door and tries to pull you from the vehicle, the seat belt will hold you in place while you step on the gas. Make sure all your passengers are belted in, too, so they don't fly into you during a defensive driving situation.

Don't leave loose packages lying about in the passenger compartment. Especially don't keep anything in the rear window well. Keep heavy items securely tied down or stored in the trunk. You don't want missiles whipping about your head if you're forced to take evasive action or crash your vehicle .

Don't let your car's fuel level get below a quarter tank. If you should happen to get into driving trouble with one of the growing number of morons on the interstate, you'll need extra gas. It'll be a comfort to know that you have enough fuel to make the nearest police barracks or to keep driving long enough to get away.

Having a little extra fuel in the tank also allows you to drive on by if a chosen gas station is full of shady-looking characters. You'll be safer to stop at the first decent station you see after your tank gets about half empty. If you pay cash in advance, learn to put an even amount in your tank, or use the quick credit card so you need not wait for change.

Where are you going? Makes no difference! Tell somebody; leave a note. Standard procedure in many households is to post a small blackboard near the inside of the front door where spouses and kids send messages and love notes. Then, if you don't return on time, your loved ones can notify police.

If your car breaks down, stay with the vehicle. Think of it as a turtle shell. If someone offers to give you a ride to a service station, decline. Hang a towel or scarf from your side mirror and wait for a state trooper or other emergency service vehicle. Don't leave your vehicle, don't get in anyone else's vehicle.

When you drive, pay close attention to what's happening on all four sides of your vehicle. Scan both side mirrors and your rear view every few minutes. Don't follow the cars in front of you too closely. If you do, you'll pay too much attention to traffic ahead of you and break the good habit of scanning your rear views.

Avoid public restrooms. Many highway rest areas are now routinely patrolled by thieves and perverts. Homeless people often live there. If you absolutely need a restroom, restaurants and truck stops are safer than public facilities. Men: Avoid urinals. You're extremely vulnerable to attack when standing with your back to the world in that circumstance. Use the toilet compartments and lock the door behind you. If no door, stand to the side. Thieves look first for a pair of pants dropped around shoes. Then they quietly climb on the seat in the next stall to check the hook. If your coat is hanging, they'll be gone with it before you can do anything.

Women who put purses on the floor or hang them on a hook run the same risk. Other females (perhaps homeless) prey upon rest stop travelers. It's best to carry a purse with a shoulder strap and hang it around your neck. Don't set your purse on the sink either. Keep it securely on your person.

Above all, **DON`T PICK UP HITCHHIKERS!** Thousands of bright people make this mistake each year; some pay with their lives. In most states it's not only against the law to hitchhike, it's against the law to pick them up. Don't be fooled by the gas can trick, either. The real criminals know how to make themselves look most pathetic.

Stranded motorists are the same. Don't stop on the highway to give assistance. Stop at a pay phone and notify the state police if you see someone in trouble. Use your CB and call for help. We can't afford to be good Samaritans on the highway. The risks are just too great. You can't risk helping a stranded motorist. Even someone lying on the road could be setting a trap for you.

All of us have long thought of our cars as private places. That's no longer true. Drivers are easy prey for criminals. But if you turn up your perception knob, make a few additions to your vehicle, and stay locked behind tinted glass, you can avoid almost all highway robbers and street thugs.

Chapter 8

HOW TO REDUCE RISKS WHILE TRAVELING

On public transportation, the sophistication of the crime goes up with the cost of travel. Bus and train stations get bums and weirdoes; first-class air fare on a Concorde might put you in the path of a con artist. Buses carry some animals you can't believe. One police search of an interstate bus recently yielded several weapons and enough drugs to fill a briefcase. On the other hand, you can be pretty sure you won't encounter a weapon on an airplane. As a general rule, cheap travel puts you at risk; expensive travel puts your property at risk.

Another factor is the crowds. With a lot of people around, crimes against persons don't occur as often. But you have to watch out for your property. If they can grab your purse or your bag, they'll disappear into the crowd and be difficult to chase.

Overall, the same defense principles you apply elsewhere apply when traveling. Avoiding crime in transit is much the same as avoiding crime anywhere—-with a few new variations on the theme.

In most tourist areas, criminals can steal property without much fear of prosecution. Hawaiian car rental agencies will tell you to leave your car empty with the trunk open and carry everything on your person.

Why? Because thieves will break open the trunk and damage the car beyond the value of the goods they steal. Car burglary in Hawaii is profitable. Even if the criminal gets caught, the victim doesn't want to fly back from the mainland to testify after his vacation. But the minute the germs start messing with the tourists, themselves, all hell breaks loose. On Oahu, two armed robbers on a backpackers' trail were apprehended. and sentenced to 24 years.

So—-tourists should be most concerned about theft. Who steals? All kinds of people, although low class, rough looking transients will be prime suspects. But don't be fooled by appearances. The typical NGHOL (Nice, Grey-Haired, Old Lady) can steal as a complete surprise, from you, and hundreds of others. They frequently have a drug crazy need for more money than a highly paid executive can make. Women with the same needs get cash in other ways, but they can also be thieves when employed as maids, clerks in hotels, etc. If you travel cheaply, then you can expect the employees of the firms you'll be dealing with to be in a lower economic bracket. Guard your goods; dress down to the level of your traveling companions; don't flash any money or jewelry. In a motel, use the safe or vault. Failing, that, get creative in the art of hiding valuables.

Once you understand that danger levels change as your modes of transportation change, you can consider some of the different ways in which you may be traveling. Then, make your crime defense plans accordingly.

ON FOOT
If you walk much and your neighborhood is rough, don't carry valuables; carry defensive weapons. Purses attract thieves like sticky

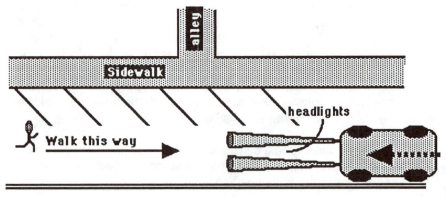

paper attracts flies. Walk against traffic. In Los Angeles during August, 1992, one of the month's 263 violent fatalities was a 94 year old grandmother with $8 in her purse. Purse snatchers in a car dragged her 100 feet to her death.

Day or night, don't walk on the right side of the road. Even if up on a sidewalk, walk on the left---**against** traffic. You're safer to walk in the middle of the sidewalk than on either edge, too, because most of the crud hiding in alleys will hesitate to run out to get you. Those who do attack can't corner you as easily as they can on the sidewalk. In addition to the above, stay on main streets. At night, don't travel where it's dark.

Dress for combat more than looks. You can fight freely and run fast in tennis shoes and loose-fitting pants. Tight skirts and high heels leave you at a disadvantage.

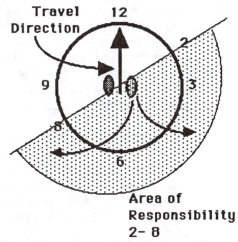

WALKING IN PAIRS
AREAS OF RESPONSIBILITY

Travel Direction — 12 — 9 — 3 — 8 — 6

Area of Responsibility 2- 8

As much as possible, don't walk or ride around alone. Many street criminals work in pairs. They have more nerve that way, and they actually fight nastier because each tries to impress the other. Besides that, they're afraid of losing. Seldom will they attack a superior number. So two or three in your group are less likely to be attacked than one alone. "There's safety in numbers," also applies to prevention. When bodyguards work a detail, each has an area of responsibility. You should, too. One of you watches the right and rear, from 2 - 8 on your defense clock. The other scans the front, from 7 - 3. Be professional; overlap.

Another great advantage to travelling in pairs: Broader range of weaponry. One carries short range weapons, the other carries long range. One carries gas, the other carries firepower. Warn each other about danger.

97

When you notice a rowdy group a block away and moving towards you on your side of the street, walk across the street or into an occupied building without attracting attention to yourself. When you can't avoid such a group, approach them with your head up and seek eye contact with one member of the group. Remain calm. Do not display fear but at the same time don't create a challenge that might require a response from them. "Dissin" is street talk for disrespect, and you would be surprised at how little it takes to incite a gang attack, especially when you're alone.

In a crowded area, prevent pickpockets from ripping you off by sewing Velcro on your pockets. When a pickpocket lifts the flap, the ripping noise tells you what happened, and tells him you know.

In transit, from bus to airport, van to bus station, etc. don't allow anyone not in porter's uniform to handle your baggage. If a stranger does handle your bags, chances are he'll run with them or extort a tremendous fee for carrying.

WHILE SLEEPING IN A HOTEL

Choose a ground floor room so you eliminate the need for using elevators or stairwells at night. On upper floors, ask for a room away from elevators. This makes the room less attractive to thieves because the escape route is too long. Don't take calls from hotel maintenance unless you get a clearance from security. Some hotel victims have let uniformed maintenance people into their room---only to find out they were imposters who first called, then beat and robbed them.

Improve security by staying in the room while it's being serviced by cleaning staff. Keep expensive cameras, watches, and jewelry out of sight whenever hotel staff are in the room. Place room service dishes outside your room and thus eliminate one more reason for staff to enter. With duct tape and plastic baggies, stick valuables to the undersides of desks, drawers or other furniture. Otherwise, use the hotel's safe.

Inform the hotel operator **not** to ring your room, but to take messages only. This makes it hard for anyone to find out whether you're there or not. Keep the security latch or chain on at all times. Leave the "Do Not Disturb" sign on the outside of the door. Close curtains on the entrance wall, especially when absent. Leave a TV or radio talk show station on when you leave. Do all of the above, and your motel stay should be reasonably safe.

98

SLEEPING ON THE GO

If you sleep while traveling on a bus, ferry, etc., sneak a secure line (parachute cord) to your pack or briefcase where nobody can see it; then tie that line off where a slight tug on it will wake you but a hard yank won't throw you off balance. Use a coin locker if you'll be spending several hours in an airport or train station. But then park your carcass where you can keep an eye on your locker. Lots of coin lockers are ripped off by people who rent the locker, then make a copy of the key.

When sleeping on planes and trains, keep tickets and other valuables in your inside coat pocket. Place your carry-on bag under the seat in front of you and put your feet on the bag while you sleep. With shoes off, you'll be much more sensitive to any movement.

AIRPORTS, BUS AND TRAIN STATIONS

Women, keep your checks and tickets in a handbag or briefcase. Shoulder bags with heavy straps make a lot of sense for the female traveler. They make it difficult for a thief to grab your bag and run. With the bag over your shoulder, then covered with a coat, they can't see your purse, much less snatch it.

Form an alliance if you're alone. Just make sure the person you pick is reliable. Choose women over men, clean over dirty, well-dressed over shabby. Recently, I flew from Hawaii to LA. then took a van downtown to catch a Greyhound bus into the desert. I was pass-out tired, and my bus wouldn't leave for two and a half hours. I saw two teenage girls with bags huddled in the corner, more scared than I. In a quick interview, I learned they were from England. They'd come here to be nannies at a children's camp, saved their money, and were touring through the USA. I needed rest so I said, "Let's make a deal. I'll plop down here and sleep; you watch my bags and warn me if a problem develops. Tell anybody who comes around that I just got out of the mental hospital in Camarillo and they should be extra quiet. If they bother either of us, I'll take them apart." The girls were wide-eyed and more than happy to stand watch. I rigged a line from my backpack to my belt loop and covered it. My tote bag was my pillow. We moved to a strategic corner, and I dreamed away.

The same general plan works in youth hostels, air terminals, on ferries etc. If more than one party has access to your quarters, and you're alone, do a little interview work and find someone you can team up with and trust. Try to make sure that one or more in your party stays awake while the other sleeps.

ON A BIKE

I took a bike ride around San Diego recently. I was a cop there and I know the city pretty well.   By talking to a lot of new homeless people who moved to Balboa park, I learned things are tough. The beautiful tennis complex where the mighty Mo Connelly trained and became a tennis star is being abused. Homeless people trash the tennis courts through the fence during daylight matches. Drugs abound. Car burglary is common. Night times are dangerous.

> Wear your helmet! Drivers on drugs don't see a cyclist, they see a bike that will get them a quick fix for just nudging you with their cars. Also, you can duck your head and thus block a lot of incoming blows.

If you pedal to a San Diego store in daylight, and leave your bike without locking it, kiss it good-bye. You can tell how many are stolen by the street price of a 10-speed. Under $15.

San Diego is no exception to big city blight. Bike riders not only need to watch their wheels; they need to take care of themselves.   In a pinch without any other weapon, your bike pump used as a pool-cue penetrator or a club will give you *some* help, at least.

If you ride alone, you can take your mountain bike into the wilderness and be fairly safe from crime. You can disappear into the woods, and nobody knows you're there unless you make a lot of noise or burn a smoky fire. You can also ride with a group and enjoy safety in numbers. But if you ride alone and travel down streets in a bad part of town or on a secluded bike path in a city park, watch your bottom. Ambush is a distinct possibility. One sideways shove and you're down. Anything more and you may not get up.

When I lived in Oregon, I used to ride the logging roads of Lobster Valley and I always carried good firepower because of the pot growers in the area. There, however, I had a chance because I was alone on the roads most of the time and could hear or see trouble. In city parks, it's not like that. They can hit you before you see it coming.

In cities with little crime, you can ride on the right side of the road. Drivers don't want an accident, and most will steer clear. Where the crime problem is real, though, ride the way you walk—against traffic. You can't afford to get hit from behind. On a country road, you can always ditch. In a city, you go up on the sidewalk or pull in between parked cars and halt.

When you ride against traffic, watch out at driveways and corners! Drivers will be looking for traffic from the opposite direction only. Wear a helmet, too. In a fight, you can duck your chin and an incoming blow bouncing off a bike helmet won't do damage to anything but your assailant's fist.

TAKING CABS

Never get in a cab unless you first ask how much the fare is. In the Philippines, the answer for fare to Clark Air Force Base was, "Oh, it's a short trip, you can pay me what you want." Then, after we arrived, fifteen Filipinos surrounded my cab while the driver tried to extort big bucks from me. We settled, of course, but I lost money.

In Spain once, the cab driver told me, "Whatever the meter says." He then proceeded to make more than four right turns so the shadows were back on the same side as they were when we started. (See Paul's *Never Get Lost*.) I got out of that cab, paid the driver, and caught another one.

When taking a cab by yourself in a foreign country, sit directly behind the driver. Order him to lock all the doors. In the Philippines and Mexico, drivers often go to a place where they meet a gang of twenty. Routinely, when I worked as a cop on the Tijuana border, we would see badly beaten sailors dumped back at the border in skivvies only. In Thailand, I traveled with a Green Beret buddy who always sat behind the driver. One day a cab driver made a wrong turn into a dark and cruddy section of town, but a very sharp 2" pen knife caused the driver to stop, back it up, and drive in a new direction. As the cab pulled out on a main street again, the knife disappeared. Later, my buddy had the driver stop in front of a cop; we got out and paid for the ride in plain sight. It was a polite encounter.

ON THE BUS

This is now a dangerous way to travel in the U.S. I always wonder about the drivers---they look so respectable. But they settled the last strike by using snipers to pepper the buses. Bus travel is cheap, which may be why the terminals are human junk yards. Some of the travelers scare me. On a bus, feel free to change your seat as the situation demands. You don't have to stay in one place. If you ride in the back, nobody sits behind you. Moving to the front may provide safety in numbers.

Bus and train terminals see lots of scams. Most have to do with ticket exchanges. Don't buy tickets from anyone but the airlines or rail ticket office. One of the most prevalent scams works like this: A presentable-looking individual will approach you and explain that his or her wallet or purse has been stolen along with their tickets. They have a Rolex or Nikon or something worth a great deal more than the cost of the ticket they need. If you're willing to buy them a ticket, they will give you the "item" for security. When they get home they will send you the money for the ticket plus $100 and you can return their property. Sure. Either the property is stolen or it's a fake.

Generally, keep your distance from strangers. Don't let them lead you into a conversation. Get tactically situated if you have to wait. Corners are good, as are seats against a wall. If you're waiting in a long line and someone scary gets behind you, address the situation. Say, "Are you waiting to buy a ticket?" If the answer is yes, say, "Go ahead of me, please. My bus won't be leaving for a long time." You need to stand <u>behind</u> a suspicious person, <u>not in front</u> of him.

With luggage in the overhead rack, you'd best stay awake. If you're really tired, move your bags to a window seat, then sleep leaning up against them from an aisle seat.

In a foreign country, buses and trains are somewhat safer. Even so, I make an alliance with somebody before I sleep. I once took my 10-year old boy on a train trip deep in Mexico through the Tarajumara Indian country. I speak fluent Spanish and made friends with a *Cabo* (corporal) in the *federales*. I taught him a few things about his German assault rifle. He taught me a few things about the absolute authority he had to shoot any suspect. We slept in shifts and I never lost a dime.

<u>A NOTE ON FOREIGN TRAVEL</u>
Assuming the purpose of travel is pleasure, why not go somewhere nice—-where you don't have to worry about crime? What

parts of the world are most crime-free? As it happens, English is spoken there. New Zealand is a country with a tradition of peace, friendliness and propriety. In Australia, I stayed in a rough neighborhood and found it free of crime. Parts of Canada are also nice—notably Vancouver Island, B.C., which is full of people who are lovely to the core. I lost my wallet on a bus there. Someone found it, turned it in, and the BC Transit people called me. They returned it with the hundred dollars and all credit cards untouched. On the other hand, some Canadian cities are now a little rough. Hawaii is not crime free. Parts of Oahu are downright dangerous. If you want to experience the feeling of a lone black person at a white country club in the South, try to surf with Hawaiian locals on their beach. You're a haole, and they may bruise you badly.

Europe has its fair share of crime. Besides, you have to hassle with the petty crooks who take advantage of the fact that you can't speak the language. In Germany, for example, a hotel added a good-sized surcharge to a bill for bathing until I straightened it out. In Italy, once, a 16 year old sweetheart of a girl shortchanged me and I caught her at it. "Mire," I said, as I held the coin up, *"Cinque, cinque."* (Look, five, five!) Oh—she was so embarrassed. She took back my coin and gave me some others, which I dumped in my pocket. "Got to get up real early to fool me," I thought. Later, after I'd left the cafeteria, I recounted the money; she'd shortchanged me worse the second time.

Mexico can be a little rough, especially in the border towns. Labor is cheap, as is life in some parts. On the other hand, country folk there are genuine. The general rule to apply when you travel in a foreign country is to look around. Your first clue: See if the bicycles are locked. In Fussa, just South of Tokyo, Japan, whole racks of bikes outside a department store had no locks on them. The crime rate there was low. Visit Vancouver Island, Canada and notice smiles and summer flowers everywhere. You don't have to worry so much. However, in Guatamala recently I went into a bank and saw a guard there with a machine gun. I spoke to him and asked why he was armed that heavily. "Hay muchos ladrones, (There are many thieves.) he said. He wore a bullet proof vest, too. Likewise, when you see broken glass or barbed wire on the top of a wall, the criminal germs in the neighborhood are restless. Be on guard.

If you want to see some real crime, visit Washington D.C. or many major U.S. cities. You can sit on a porch near the White House on any given night and enjoy the gunfire. Also, spend some time in St. Croix, U.S. Virgin Islands, where, after Hurricane Hugo, even the police and National Guard were looting.

IN THE AIR

Air travel offers fewer problems than cheaper forms of transportation. Not only do you mix 'n mingle with a higher class of passenger, but inspections make theft less easy. Carry on as much baggage as you can. Baggage handlers are poorly paid employees who sometimes supplement their income. For check in, I use cheap luggage in which I keep a candle. Drop a little hot candle wax to make a seal on your baggage locks and you'll be able to tell if the bag was opened since you saw it last. Another way, either pull a hair from your head or a match out of a matchbook. Hang one of these half in and out of the case so they barely protrude when closed. If it's gone when you land, your luggage was opened.

Overstuffed luggage is frequently dropped by handlers because they know it will pop open so they can pilfer a few items. Put an ID tag (no home address) inside your luggage. People who steal luggage around airports often cut outside ID tags off. You can identify your bags more easily with your ID hidden inside.

In the terminal, use the dining and rest room facilities located inside the security check points. Crime is less prevalent there. Board the plane early while the overhead storage is empty. Store your carry-ons directly over your seat; otherwise they may be gone when you land. Be careful about what you put in the overhead storage compartments. Someone could grab your stuff while pretending to get something out of their own gear. Put a spare toothbrush and paste, a razor, and one clean change of clothes in your carry-on baggage in case your checked-in bags get sent by mistake to Egypt. It happens all the time.

ON THE BEACHES

Buy a beach towel and a hand towel made of the same material. Then, sew the two together so the smaller towel makes a color blend-in pocket with Velcro flap on the big one. Carry your beach goodies in there. With the pocket on the sandy side, nobody will see it. Even if you have to go for your gun because you suspect trouble, it will look as if you're wiping your hands. If the trouble really develops, you don't have to display the pistol. Just shoot a hole right through the terry cloth.

Hollywood stunt woman Sunny Woods has spent more time on the beach than most other humans spend at work. She began her career as a surfer. Then she lived in St. Croix for six years. She dives, suns, plays volleyball, and jogs. Most of her life, she was on her own.

On the beach she carries her car keys, money, ID, and a loaded pistol. Even though she goes swimming a lot, she hasn't lost anything. Why? She looks around, and when nobody is watching, she buries it all a few inches below the surface in a plastic baggie. Casually, she rolls over on her towel. Then she gets up, goes into the water, and returns to the towel. After she dries off, she rolls over, sits up, and digs the baggie out. She can also retrieve it by dropping her towel over the burial spot and picking up the whole package. That allows her to draw the weapon under the towel and be ready to shoot through the material. What a pleasant surprise.

TWO MATCHING TOWELS SEWN

Two obnoxious men on two separate occasions have come close to meeting Jesus when they bothered her. But there is a sixth sense in every criminal that tells them—-pressing this is probably a bad idea. Maybe it's the way she spoke when she knew she had a gun under the towel. Perhaps it was her posture—or the way she held her head. Anyway, life goes on in the big city. I suppose they bothered someone else.

GENERAL RULES
When traveling, never carry more cash than necessary. Of course, make sure to have enough cash to satisfy a mugger. You can't afford to make one mad at you. Carry traveler's checks and use credit cards you can replace. Your responsibility for charges on the cards ends as soon as you report them stolen. You would think that's good news, but it's the opposite.

In January of 1992, I flew to New Orleans with a Louisiana sheriff who told me victims in the French Quarter were being robbed at gun point, then shot. The police couldn't figure out why. We found out. It's because dead victims can't report their cards stolen. Fences will pay a higher price because they can charge on the cards for a longer time. You can fix this for under $1. Toss all your important documents (licenses, ID's phone calling cards) and credit cards on a copier and push the button. Copy both sides. Staple the sheets together. Leave that list at home along with your list of traveler's checks serial numbers, and the serial numbers of any computers, cameras, guns etc. If you don't report in on time, have your cards canceled and the local police informed of the card and I.D. numbers. That should help lead to the bastard who blew you away. It *might* also save your life when you explain that the canceling procedure is automatic.

Never discuss your vacation or business plans with hotel staff or any other local. Many hotel employees drink in local bars and may have a moonlight job as an information peddler. You draw attention to yourself by either over tipping or not tipping at all. If you don't tip enough, you become a subject of sore discussion between the maid you stiffed and someone at the bar who's listening to how rich and stingy you are. Tip too much, and they talk about what a rich, big spender you were. Either way, you may become a target. Just tip fairly.

When planning your travels, do a little research on the local laws about weapons and defense. This is doubly important when you're visiting a foreign country. Some officials get awfully upset about an undocumented firearm.

Learn to depend on other defense measures when you can't carry a handgun. You can almost always carry a knife. Check it in at airports and you retrieve it when you land. Make sure yours opens with one hand. (See Don's *Everybody's Knife Bible.*) You can also make a Bo or a short club with the clothes rack bar out of your hotel room when you go jogging. With a saw blade or knife, you can make a decent weapon out of any broom. Roll the handle and tap on the back of a knife blade to knock it progressively into the wood and get a clean cut.

Become an astute observer and quick reactor. Be aware of everything going on around you all the time. What you train yourself to look for is something out of place or someone out of line. Long coats worn in hot summer times can mean weapons concealed underneath.

CUTTING THROUGH WOOD EVENLY

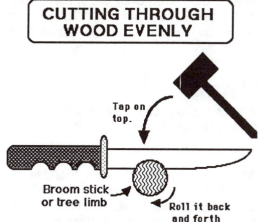

Tap on top.

Broom stick or tree limb

Roll it back and forth

Illustration above taken from *Everybody's Knife Bible.* Tapping on the back of the blade will almost give you a square cut.

Look at the pictures of criminals on TV and newspapers. Much like the elegant ladies walking Rodeo Drive in Beverly hills during the day make their statement of beauty, elegance and wealth, notice how criminals dress to make a statement of their own: "Here, I send you all my middle digit. I wear hellacious tatoos, chains and studded wrist leather. I've decided to have my male menopause 30 years in advance, and I'll dress up and stink accordingly." That doesn't mean crime can't come from a well-groomed man, but when a person makes an out of line statement, it generally gives evidence of an abused, born-for-welfare-only, bastard child, and you'd better pay close attention.

Think about what you can do if a violent situation develops. Don't let your loved ones walk into a trap. Avoid trouble. Planticipate. You're a good bodyguard when you keep out of trouble. Former cops and Karate pros are not as good at bodyguarding because they focus on getting out of trouble, then making an arrest. That's how they think. But we want you to think way ahead of that---stay trouble free always.

Don't drive away from your home city with your dealer's license plate frame on your car. They make your car a target for burglary. In San Diego, at Sea World, for example, Oakland dealer plates tell a car burglar you're a tourist---not likely to drive hundreds of miles to testify about your stolen golf clubs in court.

ON A DATE
Men, quit driving. Let the woman drive and you ride shotgun. You are a LIFO gentlemen; forget Emily Post until she learns what's right for the great society we live in. Remember: LIFO means Last In, First

Out. If you get into trouble, she should leave. Once out of harm's way, perhaps a block or so, she can call police, honk horn, flash lights and try to get some help. A shot from a gun, even in the air, will cause many perps to panic and flee.

AT CROWDED PUBLIC EVENTS

Be careful in a crowd. For the past several years I've made a point of carrying tickets, driver's license, one credit card and $10 in cash whenever I've gone to ball games or races (auto or horse). I carry this in my front pants pocket.

Ladies, don't wear jewelry to ball games or races. Blend in with the crowd. Don't wear anything or do anything which might draw the attention of thieves. Remember, employees at public events often come from a labor pool that is part time. Some sell information. Also, criminals act on victims and property targets of opportunity. If you don't present that opportunity, you may save yourself a lot of pain.

As crime becomes more prevalent, travel is riskier. Still, though, you may have to go somewhere to do something you can't do through the mail or over the phone. Apply the precautions and tricks in this chapter, and your chances of having a safe and enjoyable trip will be much improved.

CONVICT---LOSS OF RIGHT TO SUE

Why do convicted felons have a right to sue anyone? Conviction for a crime automatically has to wipe out the criminal's standing to litigate. Convicts have abused the privilege. They break in, beat up, rob, and rape their victims. If they get hurt in the process, they sue their victims from jail. They get a free law library along with all the time in the world to sue anyone for anything. Meanwhile, it robs the vitim's peace of mind, costs attorneys fees to defend, lessens the victim's ability to earn his own livelihood and return to a normal, post-trauma life, and in general, makes a mockery of our justice system.

Even if he loses the lawsuit, the convict plaintiff becomes a hero in prison. His litigation sends a message to all U.S. law-abiding citizens: "Don't disturb a burglar in your home; it may be less trouble to let him take it all."

Is there a congress person out there who can fix this?

Chapter 9

How to...
DEFEND AGAINST RAPE AND ASSAULT

The amount of rape in the world is an indicator of how far we've sunk. Our position: We wish to hold women in honor and respect. We care about women and the terrible problems they face in an increasingly hostile society.

Having lived all over the world and met hundreds of people in all kinds of settings, we are aware of some things women aren't: **How some men think about them.**

Some declare themselves "leg men." Others consider only your backside; that's all. Finally, there's the great vocal majority. You get high grades for a great chest.

What it all goes to say is this: Many criminals don't consider you, the person. An abundance of other attractive female attributes are replaced with nothing more than the male assessment of your T&A. Do you know why? Because it's demeaning. If a criminal can put you down, it gets him psychologically up. If he can admire only a part of you, the rest becomes insignificant; therefore, he's significant. When attitudes like those are prevalent in a society, women are in trouble.

THREAT OF RAPE---THE ENEMY'S MIND SET.
How did the world fill up so fast with rapists? What's the nature of the crime? What's the criminal's mind set? This is where we think a

large number of rapes come from. <u>Man's disrespect for women and the sacredness of sex, which in turn comes from the media's proliferation of pornography</u>. For this indictment, we define pornography as anything causing a man to be turned on sexually. But, arousing lust is not the prime problem. When an unbalanced person finds vicarious acceptance of sexual misconduct from television, in movies or magazines, sooner or later, he will turn to the same misconduct .

Through the media, men are conditioned to think of women as hunks of flesh, to be admired only for the size of body parts and the sexual come-on allure they can develop with cosmetics, style, speech, sway, and tight or revealing clothes. Sex without love is for men's pleasure. We teach it in our schools, encourage experimentation, and use the Playboy Philosophy to excuse our conduct.

Any society's values are represented by its art forms and you can follow the fall of the sacredness of sex as an expression of devotion by the songs we sang. From *Tea for Two, and Love and Marriage,* and Dean Martin's *That's Amore,* we drifted into Rock and Roll, (an expression coined in the black community for illicit sex). Songs sung in a nasal tone with great passion expressed every imaginable horny thought. *Rock with me Henry,* evolved into more sensual lyrics such as, *Baby, Do It To Me One More Time.* Tina Turner screamed, "What's love got to do with it?" Madonna wasn't even coy. On Arsenio, the rapper chanted, *Buns, My anaconda don't want none, if you don't have big buns, hon'.* So many rounded and exaggerated posteriors gyrated with the lyrics they should have renamed it, the Ass-sin-io Show.

Many TV shows sell sex and rebellion against traditional values. Murphy got pregnant; *Married with Children* made a travesty of the institution. *TV Guide* cited the *Miami Vice* director for pushing the sexual envelope to its limit as Don Johnson worked out over some Hollywood starlets, and the soaps played competing limbo with sexual morals, causing many to ask, "How low can you go?"

Now—-as a woman, consider the result of all of the above. For over 30 years, you've been unfavorably compared to the finest flesh *Playboy* could prop up and photograph. You and your sexuality have been the butt of widely published jokes since the fifties. A high percent of your gender were sexually assaulted as teenagers. Thirty percent of your gender lives in poverty few care about, often with children.

You see how you are in jeopardy? If you don't want to consider the effect of the media and the way it creates attitudes, try this: As men experiment with sex and multiple partners, they lose their ability to use sex as a communication of true emotional love. What men don't put out, they don't get back. No emotional involvement leads to this: many men who womanize consider themselves unlovable. Each new loveless venture into illicit sex brings the self image lower—-thus creating a compulsive desire to pump up the self image through a new sexual conquest. As he continues to conquer more, perhaps by persuasion, a promise, a lie, or by force, the thrill diminishes. But the kick in illicit sex has a measure in the mind of the offender—-it's the cleverness and power of the perpetrator added to the innocence of the victim. We think that's why there is so much vicarious thrill in porn violence; it sends the voyeur a pleasurable message, "You will love me and my sexual power *even though* I hurt you."

A rapists can be classified, as either an acquaintance or a stranger. Both are often acting out a response to dysfunction, expressed in power, control, anger, or sadism.

He wants revenge—-for the way he's been treated, the rejections he's suffered, and the scorn heaped upon him. Revenge means: He feels down; he sees rape as a way to get back up.

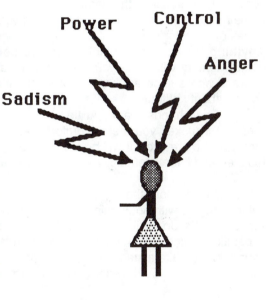

The same techniques used to defend against other types of attack often will work well to defend you against sexual assault. More than with other crimes, however, the three time elements are vital. Against rape, there are things to do **before, during and after**. What you do during each of those three time periods affects what happens in the next time period. Before is important. Since this crime is so heinous, you need to take extra precautions.

AVOIDANCE

Here's the best. Don't <u>escape a rape</u>, <u>keep out</u> of possible rape situations. Avoid suspect people and dangerous places. Since so much rape occurs between a victim and perp who knew each other, let's take a look at some new ways to identify a problem male. They act in patterns you can identify, which we list below like storm warnings. As the storm of rape gets closer and the danger becomes more real, this goes on:

Their eyes devour you. If you feel undressed by a man's eyes or frightened by the way he looks at you, take heed. Anything beyond normal visual contact should put you on notice. Be cautious with a man who stares at your body as if it were a target and who won't look you directly in the eye.

Their mouths are out of control. Look for a demeaning comment, especially with reference to your body parts. Double *entendre* is their specialty. If you took it wrong; it's your fault. Maybe it will be a series of off-color remarks about sex, your body, or even bathroom talk. Anything they put out which might be considered by some to be complimentary will make you feel more debased than flattered. Direct address words such as "broad, hot chick, sex kitten, squeeze, etc., tip you off about attitude.

Their hands roam. At first, it may only be their hand on your arm, but it makes you feel uncomfortable. Next, it's a leg. Maybe it's footsy, but more likely it will be his hand on your thigh. If you're being touched and it feels terrible, you're in grave danger of becoming a victim.

Don't ignore the signs. Rape committed by someone you know seldom occurs with no warning. At work, they call it sexual harassment; at home, it's downright improper; and from a date, it's a fishing expedition to find out whether or not you'll tolerate indecent conduct. On your failure to take a stand, at this level of intrusion, the offense will most likely escalate. If you disregard eyes, mouth, or hands, serious trouble is on your horizon.

BY ACQUAINTANCE

A rapist is an individual with a low self image. He doesn't relate well. You get rapport with him sometimes, but at other times, you lose it—severely. Sometimes he's nervous around you and you don't know why. Your sixth sense about this guy gives you a creepy feeling. Even though he appears to be normal and has a few things going for himself, something is weird and you can't put your finger on it.

Three kinds of people are: 1. those who make things happen, 2. those to whom things happen, and 3. those who don't know what's happening. If your date for the evening is the first kind, you may be the second.

Admittedly, it's hard to tell how a man may act with you in a clinch if you haven't spent time with him. Just be careful. Any man cognizant of today's peril for a woman shouldn't mind meeting you at a public place for a first date. You can take separate cars. Double dates are also a great idea. Date rape frequently occurs in the victim's apartment. Just make a hard and fast rule; admit nobody until you know them well. Before you relax and let your guard down with a date, it's a good idea to meet and spend time with his family and friends. When a man has strong ties to a family with good values, he would probably be devastated by embarrassment if he were charged with rape. Along the same lines of thought, **beware** of a man other men don't like. Just as a woman knows a woman better than a man can, men know men better than women because they relax and expose their inner thoughts more during same-gender associations.

If you have to get physically violent in order to save yourself, you made a mistake—something an aware bodyguard wouldn't do. The idea is to avoid; not encounter. If you had to pull your gun or use a baseball bat, you let your guard down, and to all bodyguards, that's a no-no. In the business we say, "dead clients don't pay." If you're going to guard yourself, pay close attention. If you don't and someone rapes you, you'll pay severely.

BY A STRANGER
Look where rape occurs most frequently.
1. In the home. Attacker hides in home or garage and surprises you. The majority of rapes occur here.
2. In a car. Surprise in a parking lot or dimly lit street. Possible abduction to a secluded area. Possibility of further foul play.
3. Outdoors. Parks. Rapists attack joggers running alone with no weapon in hand and then use bushes. After dark, early mornings are most frequent times.

You're a much more probable target when alone. As much as you can, go everywhere in pairs. If you don't carpool to work, use a dummy in the passenger seat.

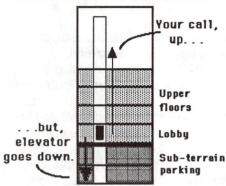

ELEVATORS PROGRAMMED
TO ASSIST CRIMINALS
IN THE BASEMENTS

Your call, up. . .

Upper floors

...but, elevator goes down.

Lobby

Sub-terrain parking

Public elevators are: human traps which move vertically between places where no help is available. Avoid elevators when alone. If you can, use the stairs. If you can't, soften your focus and have your weapon accessible. As bad as stairwells can be, they at least give you running room. Also, you have room to retreat, counter attack or escape. You're not completely cut off from the rest of the world. But to experience real terror alone in a big city full of people, try an elevator stopped between floors by an attacker.

USING THE DEFCON SYSTEM

In no other case is the Defense Condition analysis system so helpful as in the case of rape by a stranger. At DefCon #1, when a threat is 10 ft. away, you should access your weapon or look around for a weapon you can improvise, look for a means of escape, seek out a place or people where help is available, or search for a place where defense will be easier. If it's a stare in your direction you don't like, stare back angrily, defiantly, with the meanest look you can give. Don't look away, slouch, or act afraid. Even though rape is most often committed by a lone assailant, make a quick check for an accomplice, especially in gang territories.

At DefCon #2, your weapon should be pointed (under cover) at your suspect with the safety off. Also, you should be moving to safer, perhaps higher, ground. If you can retreat and get away, do that. If you get verbal contact, put it down right away. Talk to the suspect in the same tone of voice you would use on a dog. Commands such as, "*Get away from me, now! Stay where you are! Get out of here!*" all serve to provide the opposite of what a man who wants power and control is seeking. He wants to control and hurt you. When you treat him coldly and command him domineeringly, he doesn't see you as a victim. If you appear to be weak, shy or fearful, you attract him. That's why rape defense classes teach you posture, <u>head up, shoulders back and purposeful</u> ways of walking. Women who take charge stay in charge. If you're angry at the way women are treated in this society, this is a great time to let that anger come to the surface.

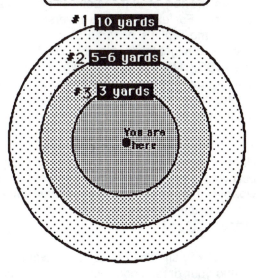

Finally, DefCon #3. The threat is close. Note here, of course, that all threats don't sneak up on you in three stages. Most rapists are good at surprise and ambush. They have plenty of time to study the area, and stalking you is pleasurable because they perceive you as helpless and in their power, (even though you may not know it). Stranger rapists often catch their victims off guard by surprise. If you're accosted, you'll have to defend. No matter what you say, scream it at him. The shrillest, most demeaning tone of voice is what you need. It's time to become 100% bitch, if you have it in you.

Once you've screamed at this person and he keeps coming on, you have a real reason to fear for your life. Modern rape includes a long term threat to both mental and physical health. Therefore, lethal force is right, as well as righteous. Once you're afraid for your life, you can take his in self defense. If you have a weapon, fire. Don't wound. Shoot to kill. It's reasonable to believe that you were so fearful, you fired several times.

But you may not have your weapon out by the time you get to the grapple stage. Hit, scratch, elbow, spit, bite, kick, gouge, and all the while, try and let the people in the next county know what's going on. Don't yell *"rape,"* either. The correct word is *"fire."* The former tells bystanders not to get involved.

Here, we need to tell you to take a defense class. But if you get good at a martial art, don't rely on it. Use the DefCon system. The problem with relying on martial arts techniques is you have to let the danger get too close before you can work your destructive magic. As General Schwartzkopf, author of *It Doesn't Take a Hero,* said, "There's always the fog of war." Lots of things can happen to you in close quarters. For example, you reverse punch well and you have a clear shot at the rapist's nose. But you miss and take out several teeth. Good, you might think. No, terrible. His teeth cut your knuckles and he has AIDS. Martial arts techniques, as well as many street fighting techniques—-knees to the groin, stomping the vamp of a foot—-all require close contact with an enemy normally stronger and more willful. Even if you think you're strong, try wrestling with a rapist on drugs.

To summarize, don't let any problem escalate to DefCon #3. Handle all rapist inquiries by long distance. Stay ready to strike. We believe: In most major U.S. cities now, if your hand doesn't grasp your weapon in your coat pocket at least once a week while your giving someone the meanest look you can, the bastards are getting too close to you.

You should be able to dress anyway you want without having to defend your dress code, but provocative dress is a bad idea. If you're raped and end up in court, some lawyer will make a big deal of how you dressed. Don't tempt fate. Don't ask for trouble. Dress for defense. Wear comfortable clothes you can move around in. Footwear needs to give you maneuverability instead of style. Our police research sources warn you not to overload yourself with packages, too much to carry, etc. Rapists are more prone to attack when they perceive you as in a weakened condition.

DURING
Judgment as to what response is best will vary. We recommend fight, scream, bite, etc, but we're not the victims and we can't tell you what to do. In some cases it might seem best not to resist. We think it's best to wait for an opportune moment before initiating a response. But the danger in this thinking is that a person may wait too long, then the possible response is ineffective.

ABOUT SUBMISSION
There is a school of thought that women shouldn't resist a rapist. Don't buy that. One, it was a terrible idea promulgated by authorities who's main motive was to keep women alive. Now, however, we are becoming enlightened and we know you can beat over half of them. Moreover, rapists are into a power trip; power to a rapist means strength

of the rapist compared to weakness of the victim. If you go weak and submit, he becomes a power, and it corrupts him. On the contrary, if you become a power, you have a good chance of winning in this situation, because encountering the opposite of the thrill he seeks (power) turns him off. **Be constantly alert for an opportunity to counter attack while the enemy is distracted.**

A friend of mine decided to become a police officer after being raped by two gang members. I asked her to speak to a self-defense class I conducted at one of the universities in northern Arizona. This was nearly twenty years ago and I still remember many of her comments.

"I've had more trouble forgiving the idiots who told me not to resist than I've had forgiving the two low-life bastards who raped me. The humiliation was worse than the physical pain, but the sense of helplessness was worse than anything else. The exam I went through in the hospital, the questioning by the police, and the reaction of my friends was nearly as humiliating as the attack itself. I decided it would never happen to me again and I would do what I could to keep it from happening to other women."

From talking with rape crisis centers, we've learned about PTRSD, Post Traumatic Rape Stress Disorders. Some victims can't quit washing, others develop jaw pain from involuntarily gnashing their teeth. Some can't sleep nights, others develop night sweats, and many jump at the slightest noise. For others, the disorders are not as severe because they fought hard, even though they lost. The harder you fight now, the easier it will be later to regain your own self respect.

WILL HE KILL YOU?
Only One Person has ever survived being murdered. Many have survived rape. As unpleasant as the whole idea of being attacked and how you plan to respond is, plan now to carry out whatever action you choose. No one wants to be raped but most would rather survive a rape than die. The time to think about what you're going to do *during* an attack is *before* the attack. In defending against rape, you have two options, passive and active resistance. Active defenses include stabbing, bruising and causing your attacker to lose interest because of a sudden death---his.

ACTIVE OR PASSIVE
Before you go active, consider passive. Passive will work for you, but you have to keep your cool. Dropping into emotional fits or

crying will most likely arouse your attacker. Small talk might keep him off balance, but don't allow yourself to be moved or manipulated into a dark corner while any stalling tactic takes place. You can try a verbal counter measure. "Here, take this money and go get a pro; I have AIDS."

"DON'T MAKE ANY NOISE."

I've been told one of the first things a rapist tells his victim is, "Don't make any noise or I'll hurt you," or words to that effect. Don't believe it. He is going to hurt you whether you make any noise or not. Make all the noise you can. Hopefully, you're not alone in a remote area. There is a chance that if you make a lot of noise and scream for help, someone will hear you and respond or at least call the police. Get all the attention you can. Screaming is a natural way to get your own adrenaline flowing. It disconcerts the attacker, makes you stronger, and helps you overcome fear-induced paralysis. It wipes out a man turned on by power. Instead of being weak, submissive, and cooperative, you become a menace; that's a turn-off.

Real active defense is the physical repelling of an assault, even if only temporarily, so you can escape. If you have a weapon, any weapon, this is the time to make it work for you. Any of the standard weapons might get you out of trouble. Add to those, hair pins, nail files, keys held so they protrude between fingers of your fist, hair spray (in the face) or high heels (especially if you're trained and can snap a side kick). Don't forget the weapons you have with you at all times. Your teeth, hands, elbows, knees and feet. While it's desirable, it's not always necessary to kill a rapist to escape. Bite, kick, elbow the throat, knee the groin, claw the eyes, swing something heavy. Inflict pain, lots of pain, then run! If you inflict enough pain a rapist is going to lose the immediate ability, if not the interest, to commit rape. If you're at grapple range, don't forget to bite. Resist with every bit of strength and knowledge, and all of the resources you have at your disposal.

Practically anything can be used as a weapon in desperate circumstances. A rat-tailed comb or any sharp object can be used to attack the eyes, throat, ear openings, or groin of a would-be rapist. With a sharp object, you can try and puncture a rapist's armpit, which will disable him quickly. Cold Steel, the knife manufacturer, offers a totally innocuous appearing hair brush which is, in fact, a molded fiberglass dagger covered by a round styling brush body. An umbrella makes an excellent weapon, especially the ones with a concealed knife in the handle.

Your kitchen is an arsenal. Serving forks, kitchen knives, frying pans, sauce pans full of hot soup, rolling pins, are all great weapons. Dozens of other disguised weapons are available. Consider each one around your home and how you would use it. Practice.

For any defense, choose a knife last unless you really know your martial arts moves, are reasonably quick, and possess an iron fighting will. Most rapists are repeat offenders; many have spent time in jail where a whole new set of sub-cultural values have been carved in concrete. A confrontation with a knife may be challenge to them; they will at least try to take it away from you. Then you have a problem. To a convict, a knife is a symbol of power.

Questions a defense attorney is going to ask you during the rapist's trial are, "If you were being raped, why didn't you yell for help?" Also, "Why didn't you resist, why didn't you fight back." If the defendant's eye has been gouged out, his ear bitten off by you, and if he is still walking hunched over a little as a result of your knee briskly and repeatedly coming in contact with his groin, neither question will carry much weight with a jury.

If you're armed, by all means use the weapon! Caution. Don't introduce a firearm into a situation unless you intend to use it with lethal results. If your life is in danger and your only choice is your own death or someone else's, let it be someone else's.

WHAT ARE YOUR CHANCES?
As a matter of fact, your chances of actually being raped are one out of three during your lifetime. Maybe one out of two, or 50%. Nobody knows. Why? Not all rapes are reported. We can understand that. First, you suffer a terrible crime; it's ignominious beyond description. It assaults your psyche so severely that the human mind actually blocks out the memory. Many never get over the trauma.

If I suffered that kind of treatment, would I report it? I'm not sure. While the laws and methods we have employed with victims (to protect rapists' constitutional rights) have become less oppressive, reporting a rape still is a frightful thing to do. You face a whole series of unpleasant tasks, from gathering evidence, to reliving the experience, to defending your honor on a witness stand before an attorney who's job it will be to discredit you.

Horrendous as the task is, not reporting a rape is one reason it's on the increase. Of course, since so many rapes go unreported, we can only make an informed guess. We think it's correct to say, between one third and one half of all women in the U.S. will suffer a rape attempt sometime during their life. The exact number isn't important; the high probability of this happening is what you must know. Therefore, resolve now to fight this. Prepare, train, and determine with your full will that if somehow you're attacked, you'll feel sorry---for the perpetrator.

REPORT TO AUTHORITIES?

Many rape experts disagree with one another on methods of escape, whether or not to submit, etc., but the one thing everyone definitely agrees on is that every rape and attempted rape should be reported to the police. As it stands, less than 10% are reported. We think that's one reason rapists typically try to degrade their victims so severely; it leaves the victim with nothing more than a deep desire to get the incident out of their mind. Also, experts agree that victims should seek immediate medical attention. As much as I'm sure you want to, don't clean up or change clothes. You've become a walking inventory of criminal evidence the prosecution will need, and without which, they may be compelled to make a deal.

> When I did the original research for *Everybody's Knife Bible*, I talked with Hawaiian prosecutors on this issue of dealing rape down to a lesser offense in exchange for a plea of guilty. Often, prosecutors agree to deal on rape charges because defense attorneys almost always threaten them with a lengthy trial. Any prosecutor's office always contends with felons' petitions for dismissal because of infringement on their right to a speedy trial. So a long trial in a rape case puts other cases in jeopardy. Defense attorneys know this and use the threat-of-long-trail tactic a lot.

You make your case stronger by reporting the incident immediately, calling a local rape crisis counselor, and allowing all evidence to be gathered with meticulous detail. We apologize for the attitudes you'll encounter in some male police officers, who perhaps have just lost everything in a divorce, or who've become hardened in their attitude because they've seen so many rapes falsely reported. Incidentally, women who falsely report a rape commit a terrible crime against all other women. Crying "wolf" is one reason true reports don't get the attention they deserve.

USING A DEFENSIVE FIREARM

Depending on where you work and play, how much you travel, whether you're out late at night, how much security you have at home, etc., you face potential rape situations. Be careful. In a situation you can't avoid or escape, don't wound. If you wound or disable an assailant with a firearm, you may make him really mad. If he survives he may take you to court or cause you to be charged with a crime.

Because wounding a rapist is such a bad idea, you need special ammo in your handgun for defense. Hopefully, this is ammo you will never use, but if you have to defend yourself, you can't afford to do an inadequate job. Practice with ammo, itself, or with cheaper ammo that shoots the same. You want the same bullet weight and velocity so you can get a feel for how it shoots.

We estimate that a majority of female urban residents who live in a major city and follow normal activity patterns face a DefCon #1 problem twice a month. Take charge of each situation long before you go to DefCon #3. Speak to the problem. With your weapon readied, but not displayed, command this threat to buzz off in the calmest voice you own. Once you've announced to a would-be attacker that you're not afraid to shoot, and the attacker still doesn't move off, you have real reason to fear for your life. Almost everywhere, mortal fear makes a strong case for shooting in self-defense.

One of the great self-defense lines was delivered by Eli Wallach in the film *The Good, the Bad, and the Ugly*. One of Ugly's early victims with only one arm finds Ugly taking a leisurely bubble bath. With gun drawn, he delivers a long spiel about how he tracked Ugly down and how he would kill him. Ugly shoots him several times with a revolver he'd been holding midst the bubbles in the tub. While putting the fourth, fifth, and sixth rounds into assorted parts of the bad guy's anatomy, Ugly delivers this timeless line, "When you gotta shoot, shoot! Don't talk!" Sage advice.

After you warn your attacker, no more talking! The key to success in using a handgun is to get ready to shoot long before being confronted. If you shoot, put in a couple of rounds, at least. Keep shooting until you're 100% positive the threat's been neutralized. Permanently! Then reload. Your having put several rounds into your attacker might well be used in court by your attorney to show how scared you were. When in mortal fear for your life, draw and fire.

The bad news is: almost half the women in the U.S. will be threatened with rape during their lifetime. The good news is: You don't have to be in that half; you can be a member of the other---untouchable half. You can apply all you've learned here; be perceptive, strong, defiant, maybe even destructive, and thereby live your life unscathed.

To make society in the U.S. better balanced, criminal courts have to change. In addition to looking at the deed, itself, they also must take a close look at the victim and perpetrator. Thus, if the "victim" appeared only to be trespassing but had a record of arrests and convictions, and the "perpetrator" appeared to be an aggressor who shot while in his or her own home, the prior-to-crime status quo of each citizen would add balancing weight to the event and its trial.

Furthermore, couldn't a judge or jury find from personal histories a certain future probability of status of each person in society? When one has been an honest 35 year old citizen all of her life, the probability of her continuing to contribute for the next 35 years is strong. On the other hand, a welfare bum with six convictions and 25 arrests during the first one third of his lifetime will probably double his trouble during his last two thirds of life.

Looking at only evidence submitted on the bare facts of a case without considering the parties' histories and probable futures tips courtroom decisions in a wrong direction and throws society out of balance.

Chapter 10

HOW TO KEEP YOUR CHILDREN SAFE AND SECURE

What makes a person become a pedophile, a sexual criminal abuser of children? The theory: They begin in an attempt to gratify a longing for love. Their desperate search is for an exclusive, loving relationship and arises out of personal emotional insecurity which may have been caused, in part, from infidelity or rejection by a former partner. A high percentage of child molesters report being a victim of the same crime at an early age. Add to that, the quest for a pure, undefiled, love (virgin young female). Finally, the fear of disease from an older lover with sexual experience makes a child desirable.

The pedophile feels drawn to be a friend of children, and often finds avocation or vocation in the child development field. Over 75% of the perps are male about 31 years old. People will say of him, "Gee— the kids just loved him."

Even if the pedophile never gets into sexual expression, he's always excited by the genuine love and concern he has for kids. They are **so** lovable—-and as his heart goes out towards them, so does his libido. If he begins to give in to temptation, he indulges only a little bit. Perhaps he tickles a child in a playful way; perhaps he fantasizes about contact as he indulges in a little voyeurism—-in child porn. Once he experiences gratification, the addiction begins.

The perpetrator descends deeper and deeper into more perverse relationships which drives him constantly to upgrade and make the thrill bigger and better. When he can't be more clever or powerful, perhaps he can find a more innocent victim—a younger child. Also, kids are often convenient victims; they're available and easy. Perhaps any young child for whom he can be the first and only lover will create the thrill he thinks he needs.

The man sitting on the park bench was of good heart, gentle nature, and God-loving. As he basked in the sun, a little girl came up and offered him a cookie. "What a precious creature, this child of God," he thought. The child's mother was nearby; she smiled. He spoke to her.

"I'm really saddened. As I think of the status of our society, I realize the nicest thing I can do for your little girl would be to slap her in the face, and snarl at her so she learns to distrust strangers. Of course, I can't do that. You'd be better off to teach her to keep strangers at a distance." He left.

Children are innocent and weak; the pedophiles who kidnap and kill them are strong and merciless. If there is crime for which all-out war is required, it has to be assault against children.

For defense purpose, we define two groups of children—under 12 and teenagers. Both age groups are at risk. That's probably because we parents trust other elements of society to provide a safe atmosphere for our teens, but they don't. To name a few—one would think the media, TV, movies, and magazines to be a decent and safe entertainment. That's not true. We think teen food is OK. It's also garbage. We think our schools are fine, but they're not. Listen to Doctor James Dobson, famous for *Focus on The Family,* a talk radio show syndicated on many Christian radio stations. He tells us with great concern about teens: "Just get them through it." That's what we'll help you do at the end of this chapter. For now, though, let's see what we can do to help your child stay alive and unmolested long enough to reach the teen-age years.

Let's focus on the little ones. One hundred and fifty thousand a year vanish. Of that number, one hundred thousand are taken away from home, school, friends and custody winner by the custody loser. Over a thousand a week are lost to strange abduction.

If you've won custody, you can help prevent kidnap by taking a photo of you and your child. If you have one, include a photo of the child's father. In a local copy shop, make several of these pictures along with a letter on the order of the following:

I'm sorry to inform you that Timmy's father and I divorced. The court awarded custody of Timmy to me. His father is **not** to pick the child up from your institution. All visitation and other child-father contact will be handled by me, personally, from the home only.

With great concern for those abducted by a parent, this book first addresses the children lost to a strange abductor. We don't want your child's picture to appear on a milk carton. If it does, we want the child found and the abductor to be put away permanently.

Huber is a very concerned parent. He writes,
"We no longer have to be concerned only with the hardened criminals and regular deviates who pose a threat to our kids welfare. Teachers, clergy, family members and older students all potentially add to the threats our children face. Our children are no longer safe in their schools, in church, in their neighborhoods, or even their own homes."

Part of the reason for these crimes is the allure and desirability of the innocence of children. I had breakfast once with a confirmed pedophile who lived in the Philippines and could therefore pursue his interest freely.
"Why do you like pre-teens?" I asked.
He became enthusiastic as he shared his excitement with me, "Because they're sweet; they love only me; they're gorgeous and they're pure."

Of course, in the U.S. men can't have open relationships with children, but the illegality adds to the fantasy—-because the child loves only him, in spite of the law.

When the threat is so pervasive, so insidious and so imminent, where do parents begin? What first steps can you take to try to insulate your children from danger?

The same threats our children face today will also face them as adults. Therefore, training about these threats has long-term value. Other threats are peculiar to one age group or another and the threat intensifies or decreases as the child grows. As the threats change, new sources of danger are discovered, and we have to adjust the lessons.

We can't keep our children in protective custody; we must allow them to experience life. At the same time, though, we're responsible for their safety. It's not easy. As defense-oriented parents, we're confident we can protect our children from most physical threats as long as we're nearby. But we can't always be with them.

Thus, teaching them to avoid or to deal with these threats in our absence is our major concern. Watch your attitudes. Make your children cautious, but not terrified. Terror leads to panic. Panic is a child's worst enemy.

HIRING A FOUR-LEGGED BODY GUARD
Prior to the time your child starts school, see if you can get him interested in a puppy. If your child mistreats animals, this trick won't work well. On the other hand, if you can teach your child to take good care of the dog, the benefits are tremendous.

You'll get a full time bodyguard who can sense dangerous situations, run faster than you'll ever hope to, attack ferociously and bite unbelievably hard if your child is faced with peril. Dogs everywhere often bite people who raise a hand to hit their buddy, a child. Also, dogs can smell a wrong person long before humans get the message.

The breed will be personal opinion. While any dog will do, we find the mixed breeds to be best. They're not inbred and therefore more stable and healthier. Also, spayed females are better than males; they don't get distracted. Working dogs, part shepherds are fine. They've been bred for the purpose of watching over sheep and goats. They herd them. With children, they often perform magnificently. We've heard stories of dogs who refused to let a father spank a child. One Australian shepherd we know comes alive at 2:45 because Sally comes home from school. He waits at the bus stop. One German shepherd we knew would growl, then bite if another kid raised a hand around her pal, Joey.

Don't let your child handle any of the puppy's discipline. But, do have the child take care of the puppy, play with it, feed it and nurture it as much as possible. If the puppy comes to your home when the child is four, he'll be the child's best friend by age five, and you should get an excellent 10 years of top-quality guard service.

126

Even with a good dog, don't rely on the animal. All of the training you do for your children and the time you spend watching them needs to be done as if the dog didn't exist. Still, if you ever slip up, the extra guard on full time duty can be worth more than all the expense and inconvenience a dog can represent.

THINGS TO AVOID

It used to be chic to dress your child well. Not anymore. We've documented stories of dead children who were shot by a schoolmate because they wouldn't give up their expensive shoes or a nice jacket. Understand that other children from different parts of your city and entirely different family backgrounds will have vastly different values. If your child is forced to go to school with another child who is looking for a way to earn some respect, your well dressed, well-mannered child is at risk.

Sack lunches made at home are best. In some schools, kids make a good living robbing lunch money from other students. They threaten their victims with a severe gang beating if the child tells. For years on end they collect a dollar a day from several victims and your child spends his academic years living in terror.

TRAINING CHILDREN

Children need preventative defense training more than anyone else because they're defenseless. They can't go armed. Teach them to avoid or escape from danger, rather than how to face it and fight against it. To fully understand the concept of training for a particular mission (in your child's case: staying unmolested and alive) read General Schwartzkopf's biography. You'll learn that training needs a clearly defined, desirable objective. So you begin teaching your children the reasons for the training. Then, conduct a field training exercise. It's like a game. You set up hypothetical situations and teach the child how to evade and escape. Long trips in a car are a good time to do this. Children are especially afraid of the dark. Conduct your training during the day, at first, then lead carefully into darkness.

As soon as you feel your child comprehends instructions, and can understand the reason behind those instructions, it's time to start his or her defense training. When children begin to accept responsibility, you need to involve them in family defense planning. Start with warnings.

Identify the various child-dangers and list the threats which apply to each area. Added to the standard, ". . . don't play with matches," expand the list of warnings to include a few more examples of the threats they may face. Again, inform; don't terrify.

Explain the purpose of the safe room or sanctuary as well as the Inner Sanctum to your children. Show your kids how you want them to approach the safe room (crawl or run) during the night if you call them. Have them practice this approach several times. Just as schools conduct regular fire drills, conduct security drills.

Teach all children to come to the safe room in your house if they encounter trouble. This is fairly easy to accomplish, even with toddlers. No matter what the problem, comfort the child in the safe room. Little Betty skins her knee and comes to you crying. Carry her to the safe room, comfort her, clean and dress the wound, no matter how slight, and when she is feeling better, tell her how safe she is in that room with you. Never discipline a child in the sanctuary. You want the room to be associated with security and safety in the child's mind.

COMMON PROBLEMS
Separation from parents when out in public.
Make sure your children can give the "911" operator their address and phone number.

Instructors who volunteer to teach hunter-safety, the course pre-required for a hunting license in most states, teach you to stay in one place when hopelessly lost in the woods. The same applies to children when lost in public areas. They need to stay put. Within a short time, their parent, baby-sitter, or teacher will discover who's missing and return to the last place they were together.

Strange cars have to be identified and avoided much the same as strange people. Teach them to avoid stranger contact and speak only to a uniformed police officer, security guard, or store employee. As you go around with your child, point these people out and ask the child to identify them. If someone other than a uniformed police officer accosts them, we teach our children to make a hell of a fuss, draw attention to themselves, and cry out "kidnap" for help. Screaming "Help; this is not my parent!" works well.

If lost or in trouble, there is a hierarchy of help your child should learn. First, a man or woman in police uniform. Second, an older, well-dressed couple. They come from a generation in which clean and decent conduct, respect for property, and love of little children was common. Third, women are more loving and caring towards little children as a matter of instinct. Avoid scruffy-looking people like the plague. Over 75% of stranger abductions are committed by males about 31 years old. We point out men in that age group often. Note this, however: People who abduct children come in all forms and manners of grooming. Scruffy looks do **not** mean a person is an abductor. Teach your child to trust nobody.

ANSWERING THE DOOR AT HOME. **NEVER!**
Whether or not your home is posted with a sign discouraging doorbell rings, **don't** allow your children to open any door for visitors. Kids are easier to fool than adults, and they make excellent hostages.

TELEPHONE PROCEDURES
Children: Don't answer the phone and give any information of any kind to anyone. Don't give out your address, where you go to school, whether or not you walk or ride, what kind of car your daddy drives—-nothing, nada, zip.

Being accosted by any stranger, either in public or at home.
Regarding strangers, teach your children to distrust nice-ness. Abductors seldom appear to be mean; most have developed a candy-coated approach to an art form. Shepherd dogs are helpful with "nice" strangers; they seem to sense who's genuine and who's not.

Being sexually molested by suggestion, touch, or request from anyone, including family members, and friends of family, and others who supposedly are in authority require the child to report it immediately.

Many cases of child abuse or molestation go unreported by the victims because children believe adults can do no wrong. Let your kids know that teachers, baby-sitters, other adults and family members can do terribly wrong things. We believe it's best to teach this: "Your body is a sacred temple given to you by God. Nobody has a right to invade it."

Children often fear reporting an adult or worry about not being believed if they tell on an adult. They're sometimes willing to take abuse, suffer pain and humiliation for years, rather than risk trouble for saying something bad about an adult, especially an authority figure. Children often sense the advances are wrong, but they don't want to cause harm to the abuser or destroy a loving relationship. Your children need to trust that you will always take their side on this problem.

Let your child's teachers and other school staff know about your children's training. If a problem teacher knows your children are not afraid to tell, that teacher will most likely choose another victim. Moreover, teachers involved in the same kinds of pursuit know and talk to one another. Once they hear about your closeness and training, your child will be off-limits to sexual abusers at school.

EXTRA PRECAUTIONS

Parents, be aware of strange people or strange vehicles in your neighborhood. Any time you see one, make a record of the license number, the make and model and year of the car, and try to get a description of the occupant. Children should learn to do the same; you can make a game out of it. If the car you suspect has bent or damaged or unreadable plates, react quickly and positively. You're never wrong to call a suspicious car into police headquarters.

Fingerprint your children. Keep copies of birth certificates, social security cards and passports in a safe deposit box. Also, starting with a child who is an infant, put together a dossier and add to it as the years pass. Photographs, likes and dislikes, fears, memory keys, speech pattern peculiarities, a five-to-ten minute audio or video of the child at play and in conversation. Make sure to get facial close-ups and pay particular attention to special marks, scars, dental configurations, and ears. Put all this in a safe place.

Also, make a list of special things only your child would remember or be familiar with. For example, what funny thing happened on her tenth birthday, something special about you or your spouse they will be sure to remember, a favorite toy or pet, or a secret place. All of this helps authorities and private detectives identify missing children, even after years have elapsed. Therefore, you'll always have hope and the comfort of knowing you did all you could.

GOING TO A FOREIGN COUNTRY

Very little can cause more panic and heartbreak than losing one of your children in a foreign country. The language barrier becomes a terrifying problem, and the police aren't too interested.

When you take your children overseas, always take a certified copy of their birth certificate along. It's also a good idea to get a passport for all of your children, even toddlers. Bring extra passport photos with you, too.

Pay close attention to their whereabouts, and make them pay close attention to yours. The rule is; <u>Never out of daddy's sight.</u>

Think about what to do if your child gets lost in a foreign country. In Mexico, for example, where could he go to meet you? Here's one plan: Type up a note in Spanish (pay to have it done) which says. "This child is a son or daughter of a U.S. police officer. Please take this child directly to Hotel Palacio and collect a _____peso reward from the desk." Make arrangements at the desk so they know to advance the money for the child's return. Place the note in the child's shoe. Train the child to give the note **only** to a police officer. Cab drivers could be trouble with a note like that if they think of a greater reward.

UPGRADING THE TRAINING

As your children mature they should become more and more a part of the family defenses. Keep on training as long as your children live at home. When they reach the age where handgun training will soon be upon them, teach safety and basics; then let them begin to shoot small caliber handguns. Games in the house played with all the lights out and the shades drawn help lessen children's fear of the dark. Night training is important because that's when most criminal activity goes on. As soon as they're able, teach them how and when to use the defense weapons in the family arsenal. Make them familiar with the alarm system and your security lighting system.

Teach your children to keep secrets. In that category will be: Family valuables, travel plans and any personal information. All that information is classified, and we keep it in the family.

Children's house guests can be a problem. Get to know the parents of your children's' friends. It's best if your child plays with others of similar values and backgrounds to your own.

TEENAGE CRIME. WHY?

As children grow, chances of losing them to abductors lessen. Other threats will pose problems as they increase in age. But early training will help them a lot because---even though a threat is one never

131

before faced, the attitude and mindset you gave your child in early years will help. Why so much teenage crime, though? Part is because teens can get away with it; our justice system doesn't punish youngsters, who then grow up with a criminal self image and a taste for evil. Part is due to the fact that so many teens don't come from two-parent families; a single mother loves, but seldom restrains with a harsh voice or heavy hand.

If you want to think about it philosophically, consider what would happen in any part of the world where humans with different backgrounds, values, and religion share common space. In early America, you could do a great job of educating students—-in one schoolhouse with a chalkboard slate. Why? Everybody had the same or similar values. Among others—-work hard, be diligent and dedicated, respect elders, and follow Godly principle.

In modern times, we think we have a better idea. Our schools are multi-million dollar educational facilities and we dedicate them. But we can't get the students dedicated. The counter-productive cloud of rebellion is ever present. Peer pressure to stay stupid and experiment with sex and drugs reigns. Weapons are upgraded. Juvenile exemptions for crimes encourage evil. Under circumstances that bad, some teachers have an alcohol problem or even take drugs.

CLOTHING TO AVOID TROUBLE
Pastor Ralph Moore (Hope Chapel, Oahu) once had to care for an errant teen relative. The first rule: "You can't wear boots and dirty blue jeans to school. You wear this kind of shirt, cord pants, and these shoes." The kid went to school. His normal choice of friends, (the hot rod set) wouldn't hang around with him because he dressed wrong. Eventually, the kid made friends with several other kids who dressed in similar fashion, graduated, and went on to college. If you let your children dress weirdly, don't be surprised if they meet some weird friends. Teach your children to go into social situations (school) with a fresh, decent, clean-cut appearance. Otherwise, they'll dress like the crowd, and follow the lead of the crowd for whom they dress.

In addition to style, watch the cost. Some shoes popular with kids go for over a hundred dollars, and could encourage armed robbery or assault. Jackets and jewelry are the same. Leave expensive clothes at home. Dressed nicely, she'll find other companions in similar styles. As parents, watch and enforce the dress code. It will help.

Normally, teen crime perpetrators victimize those with whom they come in contact. Witness black victims who die between the ages of 18 and 24. Who shoots? Same peer group. So one way to avoid serious violence is to hang around with people who don't carry weapons.

Cars fall into the same category as clothing. If the car will draw a lot of bad companions around your teenager, don't buy it. Expensive cars are advertisements at school. They announce: My family has money; burglarize us!

Brian talked about his mother's BMW because it was cool. So, somebody at school stole his keys. At 3:00 in the morning, the car disappeared; the police found it wrecked. What if the thieves had been stopped by police? With the keys, they could have claimed the car was a loan, especially with help from an attorney.

Fighting used to be a winked-at endeavor. Some parents taught their children to fight and encouraged them to do it. While it's important to teach a child there is a time---when all other options have been explored---make sure it doesn't happen often or for no severe reason. School fights today often mean severe beatings or knifings to the loser. If your son or daughter wins a fight, it could lead to fatal retaliation.

TEEN RAPE

In some areas, 30% of teen girls become pregnant, either by rape or persuasion. The problem: Many boys view rape as nothing more than extra persuasion. The street philosophy of, "anything you're not strong enough to keep belongs to me," has also fostered another kind of rape---where a male is a victim of another male.

Not only does a daughter have to avoid situations where rape might occur, but she has to be extremely careful whom she dates. Encourage double dating. If your daughter spends time alone with a young man, even though innocent, he'll be severely pressured to brag to his friends in a locker room that he made it, went all the way.

Once that story gets around, she's rapeable. Many teen rapists feel that if the victim did it with others, he's only getting his fair share. Sex with her is a way of bringing himself on a par with his peers. (Again, the rite of passage.) Also, kids know an attorney will pound on the girl's past if she charges rape. Some boy's have been known to solicit false testimony from locker room friends even *before* they make contact with your daughter. With even a shred of past indecent behaviour on her part, she could become an intended victim.

The best prevention here is caring parents who watch carefully the choice of companions, both male **and** female. Listen to Bill Gothard, from *Basic Youth Conflicts,* "Fathers, you need to interview all of your daughter's prospective dates. They have to learn that you really care about your daughter's well-being. If the father doesn't care and is unconcerned, why wouldn't the boy follow that lead?"

Girlfriends who are promiscuous will introduce your daughter to boys who expect sexual favors. While your daughter's companions might put on a great front, look for telltale signs such as provocative dress, foul language, jokes about sex, and a family background with a lack of paternal love. When your daughter's friend mentions that "she doesn't have a dad," or, "My father never comes to see me," watch out. Girls without paternal love seek it out—-frequently with older, more experienced males. Of course—-they'll take your daughter along for the ride---partly when they can get a daughter like yours to co-participate, it assuages their guilt. Witness the same phenomenon in Soap Opera popularity and tabloid gossip. If our celebrities do it, it must be OK.

SEXUAL ASSAULT FROM A STRANGER
A whole group of sexual molesters prey on teenagers. The perp enjoys making the young teenager feel guilty. The more guilt the victim feels, the safer the perp feels from report, much less, prosecution.

Most perps know that an increased degree of submission will create more guilt, accompanied by a block in memory and a severe inclination not to tell anybody what happened. Therefore, they force their victims to do despicable acts.

More than any other, this is trouble to avoid. Young teens can be lured into dangerous situations through all kinds of ads for employment. Ads for models, baby-sitters, and private help at home could all be trouble. Parents, you need to check them out very carefully. How? Get Better Business Bureau references. Talk to parents of other clients. Be happy to employ and pay 10% to a legitimate modeling agent with a history in the community for creating wholesome work.

SEXUAL ASSAULT FROM FAMILY MEMBER

For a while, this author donated time to Calvary Chapel and answered the Youth Development International Hotline. Kids under 18 from all over the country can call **1-800-HIT-HOME** for advice and referral on every kind of problem. Counselors use a giant referral book with other toll-free numbers to help kids when victimized, after having run away from home, or who are addicted to drugs or in trouble with police.

A large number of calls came from teenage girls who had been assaulted by a stepparent, an older stepbrother, an uncle, or in some cases, the girl's own father. In one case, a 12-year-old called after she had shot her abuser. In another case, a girl had been viciously assaulted by her mother's boyfriend, had run away from home, and was destitute. We called the girl's mother and pleaded with her to take care of her daughter. She refused to believe her boyfriend had committed the crime. Finally, though, she broke down and cried out, "Do you know how hard it is for me to find a boyfriend?"

Mothers who remarry, your job now is to take good care of your daughter. Watch for signs of trouble. The Bible says,"what comes out of the mouth is in the heart." A leering glance or an off-color remark are sure signs. Trouble can begin with a daughter as young as infancy. Frequent stepfather-daughter excursions away from home or extraordinary nervousness on the young girl's part can be indications. Child molestation is like cancer—-better healed if caught early—-best healed if cut out completely.

Be careful, of course, where you go for help. Some state organizations are coldly bureaucratic. Therefore, some mothers live in denial and refuse to believe children who report trouble. But if the husband has a problem with lust and you want to save your daughter, you have to act early. We recommend clergy. Church membership often helps, especially if the whole family attends together. Many of those churches teach submission on Biblical grounds, but you need to know this: You are never required to submit to sin! Your husband has **no authority** to make you submit to an evil act because God gives him **no authority** to violate Godly principle in the first place.

While secrets in a family can be destructive, mothers and daughters are far better off to form a faction against abuse than to ignore the problem. When abuse is unchecked, the daughter will live in degradation and fear. As we're learning today, the psychological damage is devastating and long-lasting. Women abused in childhood have a very difficult time adjusting to married life, and, as with men, often become abusive themselves.

THEFT BY TEENAGERS

Karl Malden should point out your young teenager and say, "Don't leave home without them." If you leave kids at home, they may have friends over. Innocent fun can get out of hand easily. We've become a litigious nation. What would happen if a teenager drank your liquor, became totally drunk, and injured someone. Might you be liable? What if someone gets hurt in your home during your absence? Also, some of the young people who visit your home may rob it on the spot or come back later for more generous portions.

How could that happen? A percentage of the students in almost every school use crack cocaine. The addiction is all- consuming. All your child has to do is make a mistake and invite one of them to your home, or let one of them crash the party—and for months thereafter, your house will be a continuing target. When they know where to go, they can't help but return for more drug-purchasing plunder. In a personal interview with an addict, I was told, "Crack is the drug for which they have a saying: 'One time is too many, and a thousand times ain't enough.'" If you want to experience some compulsive theft, let a teen on crack come to party at your house.

This is one of the worst times in the history of our country as far as danger to our children are concerned. Pedophiles are a constant threat. Perverts want to steal and kill them as young children. Peers want to rip them off as teenagers. The most insidious threat---random violence---is most difficult to defend.

If you stay physically close to them, you can prevent most of the bad things from happening. Once you develop a tight emotional relationship with your child, you can relax in an atmosphere of mutual trust. As the child grows older and leaves the nest more often, you can check up constantly on his or her companions and provide extra steerage through a channel of high morality and good values. If all goes well, you'll be able to sit back in your golden years, visit your grandchildren, and begin to worry all over again.

Chapter 11

AFTER THE ATTACK

In civil law, two citizens bring a dispute to court. One, the plaintiff, charges the other, the defendant, with the breach of a duty or contract, or payment of a debt. Small civil cases have been heard for a long time on TV in *The Peoples' Court.*

Criminal law is different, both in procedure and in what's allowable as evidence. The state brings charges through a prosecutor against suspects or alleged criminals who are considered innocent until proved guilty. Minor crimes are misdemeanors; major crimes are felonies, which in most localities are divided into Class A (most serious), B, and C felonies.

Whether you are a victim or you've been charged as a perpetrator, you'll be dealing with the State in criminal law. If you wound someone in self-defense or in defense of your home and property, you may also be dealing with him personally if he sues you in civil court for monetary damages. Don't think for a moment it can't happen. The same person who considered your home his personal plundering ground will be aided by an attorney who considers 40% of anything collected to be your loss and his gain. Therefore, wounding a criminal perpetrator is a bad idea. If you must shoot, shoot to kill.

137

In all your dealings, try to be 1. right, and 2. righteous. For item 2, we refer you to God, His Sacred Word, and His ministers, rabbis or priests.

Now we deal with item one. You want to be right. <u>Much more important, you need to think you're right.</u> If you're not sure, then you'll come into conflict with an enemy germ who will act as if they are sure (because they've already chosen not to care) and they'll shoot faster and attack more ferociously because they're more committed to battle. That's often why victims lose.

So get right. After the dust settles and the blood spills, you want to make sure you're right. The best way to do that is to apply the same principles we've laid with regard to crime generally. Your *after* depends on what you do *before*.

IF YOU WON

Be it on the street, in your home, your vehicle, or anywhere else, you came out victorious. You may not have won unscathed but you've survived. Now how do you survive the aftermath? The guilt....the possible legal problems....the natural curiosity of your friends, neighbors and family.....the unwanted publicity.....?

Your basic problem, if authorities examine the evidence, is to show that your life was in danger. If you were faced with a knife or other deadly weapon, your fear was certainly justified. Therefore, your actions will be likewise justified. It doesn't matter where the knife came from. Even if it was part of a matched set out of your very own kitchen, the fact that the perp had it in his hand (his fingerprints on the handle) will help. Your testimony (after being counseled by an attorney) that he was threatening you will also help.

WARNING

Never tamper with evidence! Even if you think what you are doing may make your case for self defense, you may, in fact, destroy valuable evidence that would have made the case for you. Forensic science is one area of the law which has improved tremendously. Some of the best police work in the country is now done in laboratories. I'm sure you've heard statements by people who want to defend their homes and are half paranoid due to the high crime rate. They say, "Heck, if he comes up to my window, I'll blow him away, then drag him inside."

138

Sorry, that won't work. Any hunter knows you can't move a bleeding animal without leaving a blood trail a blind man could follow. Even without a blood trail, footprints outside your house will reveal just how the event took place.   On the other hand, if the person lying on the ground outside your house also had a gun lying there with his prints on it, it's more logical to believe you were afraid he would shoot at you through the window if you didn't shoot first.

No matter what the circumstances were that lead you to shoot, first call your attorney. He is an officer of the court. After you've explained to your attorney what happened and been counseled, then your attorney can surrender you to proper authorities and stay there with you for questioning. This is important.

CONSIDER LEGAL PROBLEMS
Before committing mentally to shoot in self defense, it's a good idea to contact the Attorney General in your state and ask for copies of laws pertaining to self defense.

"What is it with clients? Why don't they call me and ask, 'What will happen if I slit my throat?' Instead, they call me and ask, 'I just slit my throat. What's next?'" Attorney Nelson Millsberg—-San Diego

Contact an attorney, many of whom specialize. Many law firms hire at least one criminal specialist, usually someone with prosecutorial experience. Hiring a real estate attorney to advise you about criminal law is like hiring a podiatrist to do brain surgery. Initial consultations are inexpensive; call and talk to any attorney's secretary, who will probably quote around $25. Some attorneys charge more. For example, R. Brewer in San Diego is much more expensive, but he was a federal prosecutor and often finds things others overlook.   Bar Association referrals and yellow pages are not the best referral sources. In Arizona, I once was referred to six different phone numbers, each of whom told me they couldn't help. Ask friends or business associates for recommendations.

Then visit the attorney. Perhaps take him to lunch at a nice restaurant. This is a crucial part of your defense planning. Since most crime occurs after hours, will your attorney take a call at home? Is there a special number? Will he take a call and respond immediately if ever needed? Can you surrender to her or him and let them decide what to tell the police, including whether or not you were the person who did the shooting? Discuss billing.

Since all of your conversations with your attorney are private and privileged, nothing you say to your attorney can ever be used against you. If you make a mistake and shoot too fast, your attorney's job is to see that you get the best possible defense. As a matter of professional pride, your attorney does not want to see you go to jail.

AT THE TIME OF THE INCIDENT
If you haven't called the police prior to the battle, and you won, don't call now. Call your criminal attorney. Follow his or her advice. You don't have to answer any questions from anyone. Direct all inquiries to your attorney.

Never take a chance on your police, prosecutor, or the courts. They may be—-no, they are—-often the nicest people in your community. But if you share information, thoughts, or even your grocery bill with one of them after you're charged with a crime, they will use that information against you if it will help convict. It's not personal. That's their job. **If you're arrested but not Mirandized, (had your rights read to you) tell your attorney immediately.**

If you get a Miranda warning ("You have a right to remain silent. . ."), shut up! Talk to nobody. You'll have this uncontrollable urge to explain. You'll feel a need to make others think you were right. **Don't!**

Many crooks and thieves, have foiled police; others have been released on technicalities. Authorities always need a higher percentage of convictions. Thus, police and prosecutors will use anything you say against you. When they warn you, **they are not kidding.**

Likewise, never grant interviews to the press. The press is not your friend, particularly if you've used a firearm in self defense. If the press can catch you with a tear coming out of one eye, you're news. If the press gets wind of statement of remorse, you may be history. On the other hand, if the press sees you without a tear in your eye, you were a cold, calculating, pre-meditating killer. Some relation of the deceased or their attorney can enter those statements as evidence in a trial. Generally, you're only newsworthy if you appear to have done something wrong so they can put you in a bad light. Press coverage does very little good for you. Truth in journalism is a thing of the past.

Other criminals will wonder what it was that made you such an attractive target for their deceased associate. Some of them may want to try to find out firsthand what was worth dying for. If they can successfully rip off something their former dead associate could not, so much the better for them. Fellow gang members of the deceased might consider vengeance to honor their colors.

The best response you can give to the idle curious is, " I am sorry it happened, I had no other choice, my life was at stake." **That's all.** No philosophy, no condemnation of the system and no verbal attack on the deceased. Never express guilty feelings or remorse about the act of taking another's life, not even to your closest friends. Your feelings of guilt or remorse might be construed to indicate you had a choice. Your position should always be:

1. You were faced with a set of circumstances which left you no alternative.

2. You were in mortal fear for your life and in fear for the lives of loved ones at the time of the incident.

However, don't tell anyone about your position. Exceptions: Your attorney, a priest in confessional, or your ordained minister.

WINNER'S GUILT

Even though you had no other choice and you were 100% right to kill in self defense, you may experience guilt feelings over taking another human life. Homicide is an ominous word. The prohibition against killing is so deeply ingrained in most of us that the phrase, "justifiable homicide" can cause subconscious feelings of guilt.

Here's the cure: Think realistically about what happened. In all probability, you didn't take one life; you saved several. Most criminals are never rehabilitated. They go on destroying lives as long as they live. If you shortened a criminal's life, you probably lengthened several other's. Reflect on the alternatives. How much more guilt would you feel if you didn't act positively and, as a result, some member of your family ended up badly injured or dead? The guilt over killing some felon who is threatening your life will go away. The guilt over the death of a loved one will last much longer, probably forever.

Boston news media reported this: the infamous Boston Strangler claimed he'd sexually assaulted about 2,000 women without killing them before he upgraded to get a bigger thrill. Rape is a crime

141

done over and over by the same perpetrator. Nobody reported him—until finally, nine nurses got together and reported him—posthumously.

VICTIM'S GUILT

If you're a victim of a crime involving breach of common morality or perversion, you may feel shame and degradation. That's what we've encountered with child victims of rape. Older, more clever perpetrators always manage to make the victim feel guilty because "they took part in a terrible thing." In phone counseling at Calvary Chapel, answering for 1-800-HIT-HOME, our first job was often to convince the caller that she was, in fact, a victim, rather than a co-perpetrator. Why? If someone (stepfather, uncle, or boyfriend) rapes a child and convinces her or him it was their fault, they don't tell, often for years.

Also, consider this. For years, police department thinking on the subject of rape was this: You don't die if you submit. Therefore, many victims submitted. Now, however, we've learned: Post-submission guilt trauma is psychological death. Submission helped cause an increase in that crime rate. You can beat 60% of the bastards if you put up a fight.

To help you deal with any feelings of guilt, I suggest you turn to God, the Bible and your Church. But pastors and churches are like raincoats; they do the most good if you put them on before you go out in bad weather. Life isn't peaceful anymore—principally because so many have rebelled against high moral principles. For your own inner peace, join a church. Many pastors are extremely helpful, and **they care.**

IF YOU LOST

If you've been the victim of a violent crime, knowing your attackers were caught and have a high probability of punishment is somewhat comforting. So you want to do your best to make that happen. If you lost and survived, learn from your own experience.

As the victim or witness, you can do certain things to help insure criminals will be caught and brought to justice. By doing that, you help healing, both physical and mental. You also send a message to other would-be attackers: "Crime can be risky business."

This is what to do:
1. Report the attack as soon as possible. No matter how embarrassing the circumstances, report everything to the authorities. No information in connection with an attack is too unimportant to report.

The smallest detail may lead to the first break in a case. Give detailed and specific descriptions of the attackers. Describe or show the area where the attack took place, and describe any potential witness you saw around the crime scene as well. Describe all the vehicles you saw in the area. Any cats or dogs in the area at the time of attack should be noted, too; the pet's owner may have been a witness. Maybe the kid who owns the bike that was leaned against a tree witnessed what happened, so take note if a bike was there. Make sure the time of the attack, beginning to end, is noted accurately.

2. Preserve physical evidence. Don't sweep up broken glass at the entry site. Don't put chairs or tables upright and back in place. Don't touch anything that may have been touched by the assailant(s). When the attack involves body contact with an attacker, don't change clothes, bathe, wash, or comb your hair. Lots of evidence can be found on the victim's body after a struggle.

3. Let any news release come from the police or the prosecutor's office. Don't discuss the attack on the telephone unless you know you're talking with an officer involved in the case. Never discuss the attack with an attorney who represents the criminals unless directed to do so by the prosecutor. In crimes committed by someone the victim knows personally, attorneys for the accused attacker, thief, or rapist have been known to threaten the victim with defamation or another crime in order to secure the release of their client.

Example: Rape case in the victim's home. After the crime, the rapist was subdued and captured. Prior to the perp's trial, his attorney threatened wife with exposure to husband for having carried on previous affair with rapist. Even though her marriage and reputation was threatened, she didn't drop charges. The real truth: The rapist was a complete stranger.

4. Prepare to testify in the event of a trial. Write down every detail of what happened as soon as you can. In the cases where you were the victim of a vicious or morally reprehensible crime, a natural part of healing is memory loss of the sordid details. Several months later, a defense attorney for the accused will probably use that memory loss and cleverly cross examine you to prove your testimony unreliable.

DO ALL OF THE BEFORE STUFF PRIOR TO THE AFTER

Hopefully you will never have to defend an attack. If you've followed the advice in earlier chapters, you'll see how much trouble it has been to avoid. Transcience alarms, Maxwell screens, Sabre Gas--- all of it keeps you from having to suffer a criminal encounter. If somehow they get to you anyway, though, you and your family will have a far better chance of surviving if you're prepared.

Make a list of all the defensive measures you can take now and spend the time to finish up all the details. When all the *before* things are accomplished, your *after* will be a lot easier.

Laws about using weapons for self defense and home defense vary so much that we can't report accurately. To get it right, see a criminal attorney in advance as part of defense planning. Otherwise, research the laws in your locality and for areas you'll travel through. State attorney generals' offices in each state will give you a copy of the firearms regulations. A similar call to police or sheriffs department should get you a copy of any local firearms regulations. You might also contact the National Rifle Association and the Bureau of Alcohol, Tobacco and Firearms for information on this subject.

If you can get a license to carry a concealed weapon, get one. In some states you may carry a firearm in your vehicle only if you belong to a licensed shooting club or if you have a valid hunting license. Only one or two places in this country prohibit you from keeping a handgun in your home or place of business without a permit (New York City is one example). If you live in one of those places, consider a move.

Anti-gun forces stridently protest citizens' need to be armed for self defense. Their statement: "The police are here to protect the citizens." Sorry—we don't buy it.

IF YOU ALREADY HAVE THE RIGHT, WHY DO YOU NEED A LICENSE?
There should be no license required for you to exercise your constitutional right to bear arms and no licensing entity should deprive you of a right without due process.

FROM A RELIGIOUS POINT OF VIEW

This information comes from Bible study and exogesis thereof, including original language translations of both the Old and New Testament. In addition, studies from other works are included: They are, *The Life and Times of Jesus, The Messiah* by Alfred Edersheim and Robertson's *Word Pictures in the New Testament.*

Nowhere in the Bible does it say self defense is wrong! The often mis-quoted commandment does not say thou shalt not kill; it's specific and says: "Thou shalt not commit (do) murder." Taking another person's life in war or in defense of life is not what the commandment is about. That isn't murder. Islamic, Jewish and Christian law all direct one to do what's required for self defense.

The Bible directive, "An eye for an eye; a tooth for a tooth," is not a command to seek revenge, either. In fact, it directs punishment for a crime to be in proportion to the crime committed. No directive says we must wait until a person has committed the same crime again before we act. If the crime committed is assault with intent to kill, the response commanded by the Bible is to kill in defense.

Another misquoted and misunderstood verse refers to turning one's cheek. Jesus was talking there about an insult, more likely verbal than physical. He was preaching brotherhood and tolerance, not stupidity.

One thing certainly is meant by Jesus: Personal revenge is taken out of our hands, and that applies to lynch law. Aggressive or offensive war by nations is also condemned, but not defensive war or defense against robbery and murder. Jesus admonished us not to over-react to a slight, non-lethal attack. He does not teach us to take a fatal blow without raising a hand in our own defense.

All that is righteous proves this statement. You have a right, even a duty, to defend yourself with appropriate force.

When you use that force, you not only extend your own life, but you probably save many other lives who would have come in contact with this perpetrator but for your intervention. If you do intervene, you do all of decent society a favor.

WELFARE—-FUNCTION OF CHURCH—-NOT STATE

Scripture says that if a man doesn't work, he shouldn't eat. But our government got a better idea. They teach: Welfare recipients have rights to "entitlements." The rich can pay for the poor. We can take from the haves and give to the have-nots. Does welfare work? If so, we should award the prize money to the fighter who loses, a trophy to the runner who comes in last, and oscars to the worst actors. As obvious as the folly proves to be, we are creating a nation of losers. Students don't try because they can eat without working. Children to whom welfare gives the gift of time use it to commit crimes and take drugs. Greed robs the system. Is charity a function of a merciful church or a governing state? If charity were given back to the church to administer, the state of society might be a lot better off.

148

SECURE FROM CRIME
Box Additions Index

Box Additions are inserted in the text to give the reader's mind a pause---to refresh concentration on the main topic.

Topical Index

a

SECURE FROM CRIME

Glossary

Baggie. Usually zip-lock, to hide auto registrations in trunk, and guns under sand.

Bullet. What comes out of a cartridge case through the barrel when fired.

Cartridge. Case---with primer to ignite, plus powder to propel and bullet to fly.

Case. To inspect and investigate potential theft or burglary victim.

DefCon. Short for Defense Condition, it's a new system to help you confront danger before it becomes a severe problem.

Energy. Amount of force conveyed to target by projectile.

Germ In this book, a human who infects society by preying on innocent victims.

MACE. Common variety of tear gas spray. New versions add pepper and blind the perp.

Makiwara. Japanese name for short, fist-length, fighting stick.

MP. Military Police person.

Mr Colt. Name of early American firearms inventor.

NAS New American Standard. Version of Bible popular with many because it's easy to understand.

NCIC National Criminal Identification Center

PD Police Department. Normally preceded by other letters, such as M, for Miami PD.

Perp. Short for perpetrator---one who commits crime. Commonly used by police.

Ruger. Master designer of super-quality firearms known all over for reliability and performance.

Sanctuary. Safe room in your house. Name came first from use of church to secure fugitives from persecution.

Smith & Wesson. Old and popular American Firearms makers mostly handguns.

Snuff. Real murder of a woman or child in a pornographic movie to increase voyeurs' thrill.

Path Finder Publications

1296 E. Gibson Rd, Suite E-301, Woodland, CA 95776
Other books we publish
<u>Tear out or copy this page and send with order.</u>
Check Selections

Everybody's Knife Bible. $12.<u>95</u>. Landmark book on new, outdoor knife uses. Outdoor Life Book Club selection. *American Survival Magazine* said, "...16 of the most innovative and informative chapters on knives and knife uses ever written." Just under 30,000 now in print.

Never Get Lost. $9.<u>95</u>. Best and most simple land navigation system anywhere. We've sold over 28,000. **Throw out your maps**; go anywhere you want, then bee-line back to your starting point without having to back track. System also works equally well in darkness. You can send two separate vehicles in two separate directions with no maps and have them meet anytime, anyplace.

24 + Ways to use your Hammock $4.<u>95</u> From crabtrap, to gun rest, to camouflage ghillie suit. No kidding; we really figured them out.

Everybody's Outdoor Survival Guide. $12.<u>95</u>· More innovations. Teaches exclusive outdoor know-how found nowhere else. Long range and defensive platform accuracy shooting. Animals for survival. Hand to hand combat principles, water purification, <u>plus</u> a lot more.

Great Livin' in Grubby Times. $12.<u>95</u> More advanced firearms and survival, including weapons selection and team defensive shooting. <u>Our big seller</u>, now in 3rd edition. Contains popular info from Green Beret Brian Adams on Escape and Evasion.

How to Write a Book in 53 Days! $14.<u>95</u> Tips and tricks on high velocity authorship. Power writing with data based humor and speed. Step-by-step speed writing. Automatic glossary, index and cover production. This book will save hours for any writer, new or old.

Use check overside as cash and subtract $3.
Add $1.35 for Shipping & Handling.

DISCOUNT COUPON

Tear out this page or copy it on a Xerox. Use this discount coupon to order any of our books on the other side of this page.

From

Pay to the Order of: Path Finder Publications **$3.00**

Three Dollars and No Cents

For:

Path Finder Books are guaranteed. If your book suffers water damage, fire, or consumption by goat, we'll send a new one for half price.

When ordering, add $1.35 for shipping and handling after deducting the discount amount on the coupon to the left.

<u>Dealers and book stores</u>: Please accept this coupon on any of Path Finder's books. We guarantee to redeem this for you in keystone product.

Path Finder Publications
1296 E. Gibson Rd, E-301
Woodland, Ca. 95776